Praying Naked:

*The Bare Truth about Prayer,
Hypnosis, and Observation*

Dr. Austin Ray

theHypnosisOfficeOnline.com

Praying Naked: The Bare Truth about Prayer, Hypnosis, and Observation

Dr. Austin Ray

ISBN-13: 979-8-9889444-0-9

Dr. Austin Ray
Prism Trail Press
119 Pullman Ave.
Hot Springs National Park, AR 71901

Dr. Austin Ray is available to speak at your event on a variety of topics. Email author@theHypnosisOfficeOnline.com for booking information and availability.

No Religion Required!

What if you believed in God but had never heard of a religion? How would you define your God? How would you communicate with It? The insights within this book offer a perspective on the divine creativity of God that is more in line with science. God is no longer a conceptual entity "out there" to be sought, searched for, aligned with, or on a path toward. Instead, It is present and creatively enveloping you at every moment. Within these pages, you will discover how you're already in constant communication with this divine Intelligence, and, more importantly, how you can become better at speaking Its language. You'll no longer need traditional, self-limiting, religious terminology like "Lord" or "Master." Now, you can begin to experience a more meaningful, positive, and life-affirming connection with your Higher Power.

Few endeavors carry as much significance to molding your life, as the sculpting of your self-beliefs. Central to this pursuit is forming a clear, credible, and logical concept of God. Equally significant is how you communicate with this divine force. Every success-oriented program, be it the teachings of Napoleon Hill, Tony Robbins, or the principles of Alcoholics Anonymous resonates with this truth.

This book is your opportunity for a deeper understanding of God and how It creates your experience of the world surrounding you. While remaining respectful of all religious texts, this author recognizes that God is alive in every human, not in a book.

What others are saying about this book

Praying Naked gets to the essence of what it is to know, feel, and lean into the omnipotent, omnipresent, and beneficent creative intelligence and Presence many call God, well beyond the limitations of traditional religious teachings. If you're looking to come into an authentic, personal relationship with "the God of your understanding," start with this book.

Dr. Michael Bernard Beckwith
Founder & CEO, Agape International Spiritual Center
Author, *Life Visioning* and *Spiritual Liberation* & Host,
Take Back Your Mind Podcast

Dr. Austin wrestles successfully with ways to speak of God beyond traditional "godspeak." His discussion is insightful, helpful, thoughtful, and theologically directional.

Fred Heifner, Th.D
Virginia and Guy Thackston Professor of Liberal Arts
Cumberland University

About the Author

Dr. Austin Ray is an expert in using hypnosis to assist his clients in creating changes in their emotional and physical habits, leading them to happier and more fulfilling lives. He maintains his hypnosis accreditation through the International Certification Board of Coaches and Hypnotists. He holds a master's degree in religious education from Southwestern Baptist Theological Seminary in Fort Worth, Texas, and a doctorate in consciousness studies from the Emerson Theological Institute in Oakhurst, California.

While living in California, he maintained his license as a certified prayer practitioner at the Spiritual Center of the Desert in Palm Desert. Additionally, in his younger years, he enjoyed a highly successful career as an entertainer, headlining a spectacular review at the renowned Stardust Hotel and Casino, and serving as a master of ceremonies for the world-famous Chippendales. He now resides in Hot Springs National Park, Arkansas where he is an avid hiker.

For more information, please visit his website at:
www.thehypnosisofficeonline.com

Praying Naked:

The Bare Truth about Prayer, Hypnosis, and Observation

Table of Contents

Introduction

What kind of underwear do you think God is wearing right now? Is God male, female, or gender fluid?

It seems absurd, but it's a fair question because religions use pronouns. By using pronouns, we dress God in articles of clothing and create expectations of "Him" because of what "She" is wearing. The fig leaf, the tighty-whities, or the brazier actually dresses us and our ideas about God—totally covering any possible truth we can know of God. The pronoun is the beginning of how religion clothes God and, by doing so, creates an entire religious closet for us to wear. Are you ready to take it all off? Are you ready to stand before God completely naked of religion and pray? That requires an open mind and new ideas. If you are ready, read on.

The world around me is science. It's intellectual and based on fact. Well... that's true until I'm talking about God with the traditional sources of information—churches. And then, as a believer, my duty is to stop asking questions and stay as ignorant and oblivious as possible. Follow the rules.

Don't expect consistency; instead, expect to ignore logic, follow illogic, and be satisfied with inconsistency. My role is to play dumb because that's rewarded as an act of faith.

Aunt Sallie was 32 when she died of cancer. "It must have been God's will." However, Aunt Bessie was 32 when she was healed of cancer. "Praise you, Lord; you are faithful and worthy of praise."

How can two such opposing responses be justified in logic? God is worthy? Aren't we the ones supposed to be in a state of worthiness? I'm confused. But that confusion presents the opportunity for the ultimate answer, "You just have to accept it in faith, then you get to go to heaven when you die."

I'm someone who really does love God. But how do I turn my back on the advances of science, the study of human psychology, and the development of modern culture while trying to define my life by what others tell me is the truth? Especially when they're interpreting their "truth" from one collection of books that was written by one society in the fourth century. Also, those fourth-century people don't share all my values. They considered women property and openly embraced slavery.

I've learned in life that you get to choose what you believe about God. You can embrace an idea, or you can release it. There's plenty of tangible danger in this world that I can be afraid of; there are real-world material and physical encounters that can be deadly. I've made the choice not to add God to that list of dangers, especially when I have no real-world material or proven reason to do that. The only reason I have to fear God is that someone else told me I should. That's not reason enough.

I don't know about you, but I'm completely worn out by the culture wars surrounding God. I am a believer, but any group of people claiming singular ownership of God makes no sense to me. Especially when, much of the time, what they propose seems cruel and unloving to anyone not in agreement. That's not what I'm looking for in a definition or experience of God.

I love the mushy sweet hearts of the people who label themselves only as "spiritual." And yet, being blown around by different and opposing spiritual ideas can be like a leaf in a tornado. That is also not satisfying to me. I want a God that makes sense, is consistent, and has some logic while also remaining miraculous with a mystical air surrounding It. I thought that maybe I was asking for too much until I dipped my tiny little toe into the giant world of quantum metaphysics. Instead of searching for God beyond the Universe, out there, I turned my eyes toward a quantum level of existence, in here. In order for God to be infinitely outward, it must be infinitely inward. For me, quantum metaphysics gave God a home.

I have never been interested in controlling other people's lives. I don't believe God blesses any one nation. I don't believe God has favorites, or a people, or a bride. I am not interested in creating a set of societal rules for others to follow that demonstrates they're like me or think like me in order for us to receive a Godly blessing. I don't need that. I've always wanted to control and change my own life and to have my own inner experience with God.

When I began to study hypnosis, I started changing, and I suddenly realized I was actually praying. But in hypnosis, I was reframing my life as if the change I was seeking had already taken place. Then I remembered Mark 11:24, "Whatever you ask for in prayer, believe that you have received it, and it will be yours." When done well, hypnosis assumes the change has already happened.

Although "personal relationship" is part of the religious language I often hear today, that is not the experience that plays out in our culture. When I turn on the news and hear about the religious struggles in society, it's never about someone struggling to control their personal self or the challenges they're facing with a personal relationship with Christ. Instead, the playing out of our religious culture is always focused on forcing someone to live by another's prescribed morality. It has even advanced to religious demographics, changing national and state laws in an attempt to force people into compliance with their religion. What happened to personal relationship?

I'm tired of those claims about God. I've given up on the traditional titles, the traditional roles, and the traditional sources. I want a world where each individual understands God from their own perspective and works to make their own personal life better. If each of us is creating a better personal world, then the world at large around us naturally becomes better and better. I want a world where the concept of God creates calm, peace, and harmony instead of cultural war. You may say that calm, peace, and harmony are the goals of every religion. But that's not true as long as every religion claims to be the only true religion. Claiming a singular version of the ultimate truth is just a way of declaring war on someone else.

I realize that simply by writing that last sentence, I'm placing myself at odds with most of the world's religions, especially the dominant ones here in the United States. But at this point, I just don't care. I'm not here to apologize or try to convince any reader on any point. I'm here to share with you what I have found and how meaningful it has become to me. I'm not interested in starting a religion or movement; there are plenty of those. I'm only here to present to any reader who is curious and has an open heart that there is a God. It is involved in your life. There's no need for you to seek God's will because your every breath is just that. It doesn't have to love you because It is love, and you are It. You are Its hands and Its heart. You get the opportunity every day to be Its expression of love, hate, or indifference. That's how important you are.

I love the wisdom and values that are found in tried-and-true old-world philosophies. But I also love the advances of modern technology, advanced cultures, and new wisdom. In order to create this kind of balance in a spiritual quest, I've had to strip myself of all religious affiliations, take off all my own religious clothing, and be naked and comfortable questioning everything. I've had to read anew, study anew, and fall in love with God anew.

Writing this book was an opportunity for me to tell you what I've learned in this process of ignoring superstitious fear and cultic dogma. I read books and articles about the body and the brain and how they're all so miraculously connected. I've pondered questions others ask from a scientific, theological, and metaphysical point of view. In all this study, I've discovered a sense of power that I can only think of as "higher." It is a higher power that is beyond cultural rules, even beyond what we consider morality. It's a power that's intelligent and observant and responds to us as observers. It responds to your thoughts and emotions. It is creative, and It is the basis of all life, all creation, All-That-Is.

This higher power is the medium through which the wisdom of the ages can fully express itself as good, as love, and as loving. It is inclusive and has no concept of what we consider dissimilar. It has no pronoun, no race, and expresses as the entire spectrum of light—not just what we see in the rainbow. Is that what you want? Is that what you're looking for? Does that feel like a better definition of God?

Then join me because I have found that It is Energy that I can stand in, stripped down, fully naked of any religious attachments, and pray.

Chapter 1

In the Beginning

I'm always naked.

It doesn't matter the different suits, jeans, T-shirts, or sequined G-strings I've worn to cover my body; underneath it all, I was still naked. In truth, I'm naked now as I write this. No amount of costuming will ever truly cover our nakedness. We wear clothing for many reasons: protection from the elements, the demands of society, and partly out of a need to express ourselves.

I'm always naked.

My spirit, my self, my being, my soul, name it what you wish, was born naked. Granted, most of us were born into some cultural system that included a particular religion. And that religion began to clothe us early on with its scriptures, teachings, traditions, beliefs, and convictions. But at some point in our lives, we step beyond what we were born into and into responsibility for ourselves. We either continue on in the cultural or religious system that we were born into, or we choose something new. We base our decision on many reasons: the elements of our society, the demands of our culture, and this great desire to connect with some power greater than what we perceive to be our own.

I'm not good enough. I know I can never be good enough. I don't know why I continue this charade, but what else is there?

I've had those thoughts over and over. I was usually strong enough to put them away when I needed to toughen up and meet the responsibility placed in front of me. But at some point, week after week, year after year, this great desperation would well up inside me to feel connected to a higher power that I would call God. But I knew I couldn't rise to the standards of what my culture and the religion within that culture had defined as necessary for me to have that connection.

I would sometimes have brief moments of belonging. And sometimes, I could even create longer periods where I really felt I was doing the work necessary to generate the spiritual connection that I desperately wanted to feel. There were other times when I could close my eyes and fall into the music at a church or a concert and, for a brief few moments, feel a rush in my spirit created by the rhythm and the vibrations of the sounds around me. For those brief few moments, the music would give me that feeling that I longed for—of my spirit rising to something greater. I could hold on to those feelings in that moment and sometimes even manage to hold them long enough to get to my car. But once outside the vibrations of the music, I would slowly start to hear that age-old whisper, "I'm not good enough. I know I can never be good enough. Why do I continue this charade?" The ecstasy I felt inside the church, inside the concert, inside the music was never sustainable.

Hiking in nature had become one of my salvations. Travel was a benefit of the work I was doing, and while traveling, I would often take hikes. I lived in the desert in Southern California, and my desert was rocky and mountainous. Hiking in the desert in the dry, arid air could be dangerous but also exhilarating. Leaving my home early in the day and hiking up a rocky mountain with not a tree in sight, except for the palm trees I just left at the bottom, would give me glorious morning vistas that seemed like a peek into the possibilities of the future. These moments gave me strength and stability. When traveling, my hikes were always very different and even more exciting. I might be hiking to the castle ruins atop the steep mountain in Kotor, Montenegro, or across some marshy wetlands to a waterfall in Iceland. I would sometimes hike to Lower Dewey Lake outside Skagway, Alaska, and sometimes to a quiet little dock that I knew of sitting on a calm bay in American Samoa. These hikes always brought me closer to that higher connection, just like the ecstasy of the music in church, but the feelings I got from hiking were a little more sustainable. Why?

When I was hiking, I would get ideas and solutions to problems that would seemingly come out of nowhere. In the past, I would get on my knees and beg God to give me an idea or a solution for a problem. I would try to do all the things that my religion required. I would tithe my money, expecting the miracles that the preacher promised. And most of the time, I was left feeling disappointed and, even worse, inadequate and undeserving. The disappointment was heartbreaking because I was, and am even more today, a believer in God. In my heart, I knew the feelings I got on my hikes were more than just false spiritual highs from seeing the "glory and majesty of God's creation." I knew that something really was happening to me on these hikes. It was something that would nearly always happen to me when I was alone and hiking. It was a spiritual feeling—a connection with God—that I could duplicate, reproduce over and over, and hold on to much longer. What was it that was so different?

When I go on a hike, something happens to me physically. It doesn't matter if the hike is in the quiet of a deep majestic forest, along the banks of a glorious lake, or through the loud city streets of a busy metropolis. It happens. I fall into a physical rhythm of movement, combined with a level of concentration, that puts me in a light state of trance. It's a trance that we all experience at times on a daily basis. We might experience it while watching television, a movie, or driving. I go into a light state of trance where I'm disassociated from everything externally happening in my life except the task at hand. I am focused. And in that light state of focused trance, I feel peace. It is in peace that solutions and answers come to me, not in begging and despair. It is in peace that I find health. It is in peace that I am able to find solutions and create the changes I desire in my life. It is in peace that I am finally naked.

In the Bible, Genesis 2:25 reads, "Adam and his wife were both naked, and they felt no shame." Can you imagine? Oh, for how many years did I yearn for the feeling of simply standing before God completely naked and feeling safe and loved? I ached to stand before God with no shame and no knowledge of good and evil. To stand before God and feel loved and to be able to love without bounds or conditions. My soul was starving to simply be able to stand before God and be me without pretense, without fear, without self-prejudice, without ritual, without sacrifice, without tithing, and without the clothing of religion. Have you ever felt those feelings? I kept wondering, "I have so many things about me that I want to change, and I need help with. How can I possibly pray for these things that I need while carrying around all the guilt of my sins which other believers consider unforgivable?" Have you ever wished for the peace to be able to simply close your eyes and be naked before God?

I am a man of faith. I am a firm believer in a Consciousness that I call God. I'll go much deeper into that later in the book. But what I discovered on my hiking trips was that I could go into a relaxed and untroubled trancelike state that gave me access to a consciousness where I felt at peace and where I felt naked before God. However, I can't continuously go on a hike a couple of times a day when I want to access that undisturbed consciousness. How can I find that creative and peaceful trance that I get on a hike without the hike? And then I found the power of hypnosis.

For me, the great blessing of hypnosis is its freedom and disassociation from any religion or belief system. Some people want to categorize hypnosis simply as guided meditation. And yes, it has its similarities. Hypnosis can even be used as a tool to create a deeper level of meditation if that is what you want. Although the idea of meditation is mentioned in the Bible, it is mostly in the Old Testament. And the proposal of a daily practice of meditation is more strongly rooted in both Hinduism and Buddhism, so it too has religious ties. Lastly, meditation is usually considered a passive state of consciousness where the purpose is to let go of all attachments. I wasn't looking for ways to let go. I was looking for ways to create: to connect with ideas and

11

concepts that were beyond my brain. I sought to communicate with a higher Consciousness to find solutions for my daily living and to help me live a better, kinder, more productive, and loving life.

Studying hypnosis has done that for me. In this book, I will be comparing hypnosis and prayer. I will show you how to use hypnosis in a prayerful way to be able to break emotional patterns that, over years of use, have become emotional habits. Habits are not choices; they are the opposite of choice. The tools of hypnosis can empower you to regain control to choose how you want to feel in any given moment. I will demonstrate how you can use hypnosis techniques in a prayerful way that will naturally deepen your spiritual connection.

I am a gifted musician. I made my living for several years performing on cruise ships. If you wondered earlier what kind of career would offer me the opportunity to hike in such exotic locations all over the globe, now you know. When I'm performing on stage, I go into what many performers call "the zone." When I know my material and am confident in my abilities, something just takes over my entire being, and I physically become that performance. I know I'm not alone in this experience. Many performers talk about this.

Florence Welch of Florence and the Machine was giving an interview in *Rolling Stone* magazine when she talked about going into a trance state before each show, and then when she hits the stage, sometimes she just "zones out." She said, "I have to start giving myself over to whatever it is that's in charge of performances—the performance spirit or whatever the f*** it is. I don't know because it's not really me." She added that she "always feels like there's some sacred ground on the stage."

And, of course, it's not just musicians who go into a trancelike state. Many athletes talk about going into "the zone." Actors do it. Surgeons do it. Even my mother, when she is sitting at her sewing machine and creating the most beautiful quilts you will ever see, goes into a zone that allows her such concentration on each stitch.

What if we could access that same zone, that same trance state to use in other areas of our lives, and create the changes we desire? What if we could do it on purpose? What if we could sit down and utilize that state to feel differently about our bodies, to know what's going on with our bodies, to assist with our own physical healings while seeing a doctor, to have a better mental state in our job or career, to develop greater skill in something we love, to heal our own psyche from our daily traumas, to forgive our neighbors, and to love our neighbors? What if we can simply use this as a means to a more meaningful life? What if we could use hypnosis as a way to come before God, naked... and pray?

I'm a Southerner. I was raised in the Baptist church, went to a Baptist university, went to a Baptist seminary, and eventually became a Baptist minister. When I was in university, I took a pastoral ministries class as an elective. It was an elective for me because I was actually a music student, and I intended my ministry to always be through music. In the Baptist faith, when it comes to baptizing, there is only one way to do it. You get dunked. Sprinkling a little water on the top of your head doesn't count where I come from. My folks felt that baptism—just like sin— comes from the bottom up. Your feet have to be standing on the bottom of that river or a dunking pool if you go to a fancy church. You have to get your whole body down in that water, and then the pastor has to push you even further down under, and I mean all the way under. That water, which is usually cold, has to go all the way over the very top part of your head. And if he feels it necessary, he might just hold you down there for a few seconds! If you are a Baptist, you know you have to be fully and completely submerged to have your soul washed clean! You have to be dunked and dunked good.

In my elected pastoral ministries class, there was a segment on "How to properly perform a baptism." There were twenty-seven of us in that class, and those young men were all excited to practice baptizing because they certainly wanted to get it right. They believed they had souls to send to heaven and lots of them. They were planning on sending so many souls to the sky that not only would one of those heavenly streets of gold be named after them, but certainly, there would be entire subdivisions bearing their names. Of course, in the act of baptism, there is the dunker, the pastor, and the dunkee—a newly saved soul. Since I was the only music student in the class and it was deemed that I would never have a proper reason to be a dunker, I was chosen to be the dunkee. I was dunked thirty-two times that day. There were only twenty-six dunkers, but a few of them didn't feel they had gotten it right the first time. And I think a few of them had righteously discerned that I could use a little extra time under that water anyway.

I was never a hard-line Baptist—not like the black-and-white world I see in that culture today. If you know me well, you know I can sometimes cuss like a sailor, and a dirty joke might be close to my lips. I always saw gray because I always felt like I was gray. I had a sin in my life that was a secret—that I believed was born in me—that no one could know about, not even my family. My only hope was that God saw gray too. But being Baptist was what was important in the culture of not only my family but also my town, my county, even my state. It was what I was born into. It was all I knew, and so it was what I accepted. That's not true for me today. Not only do I now see gray, but I see an entire rainbow of color in the faith spectrum. I've dipped my intellectual curiosity into other systems of faith and theology. I've read a little bit of science, and I certainly love to observe the great creation, learning as much as I can. I have studied, and I continue to study, the human psyche and condition with love and fascination. I love to take the basic principles of love that I find in all of it, and especially the Bible, and apply them anywhere I can in my life. I pray a lot. You might even say I'm a full-time prayer, but you don't find me bowing my head often. Prayer is different to me now. In 1 Thessalonians 5:17, the writer tells us to "pray without ceasing." I happen to believe that our every thought is some form of prayer. Gratefully some thoughts are more powerful than others, or I'd have some dead neighbors! But it is our thinking, our praying, that forms the life we live in this world. I've discovered that through hypnosis, I've learned to think better and to pray more effectively.

In this book, I will explore these ideas with you:

- The brain—do I live there?
- What is Consciousness?
- What is the quantum mind?
- What is hypnosis?
- What hypnotic techniques does the church already use?
- Can hypnosis be another form of prayer?

I will bring to light how many churches, throughout their meetings of worship, use techniques that are hypnotic in nature. I will point out the exact similarities between hypnosis and prayer, and in doing so, I will demonstrate the effectiveness that hypnotic techniques possess. These techniques can make personal prayer more powerful and life-transforming. My intention is to strengthen and encourage both the fields of hypnosis and prayer as powerful and viable means by which people can create significant changes for good in their lives—irreversible changes and transformative changes into a higher sense of consciousness.

Who is the one person in the world you have the greatest power over? The answer to that question has to be you. You are the one and only person that you can truly control, modify, change, excite, calm, and transform. How? That seems to be the question of the ages. You are here, alive and thinking. Each thought, and especially the choice of each word, leads to the actions you take. These thoughts and words have a transforming effect on your life that is so commonplace that you overlook it. Your power is hiding right in plain sight, as visible as the comfy couch where you sit and watch television. Repeated thoughts and words become habitual and hypnotic in nature. You already use hypnosis every day. You can use it better. By reading this book, I believe you can start to use it more and more for your good and not your detriment.

Let me demonstrate.

Chapter 2

Resistance to Different

"Well, if it's in the book."

She actually said that right to my face. This was an important woman to me in my high school years—a woman who had shown love to me, and that young man in me still loved her. I had spent countless hours at her house after school with her son. I thought she would be someone who still loved at least the memory of me enough to show some compassion. It became clear that I was wrong. She just looked at me, turned, and walked away, smugly saying, "Well, if it's in the book." The icing on the cake was the slightest little pursed-lipped, two-grunt giggle ("mhm-mhm") that added a splash of sarcasm to her words. My face was red with a mixture of emotions: disappointment, sadness, anger, disgust, and fear. And none of those emotions were aimed at her. No, they were all aimed inward at me. In our brief few seconds together, I saw myself as she saw me. All she had to say was, "Well, if it's in the book... mhm-mhm."

I rushed back to my car and sat there. My face was stinging, and my ears felt like they were glowing red. I closed my eyes, and I went deep inside. My heart was pumping, so I calmed it first with a couple of very deep and very slow breaths. Nothing was chasing me. I was not in danger. After about a minute of mindful breathing, I got my heart rate under control and forced a smile on my face. I know enough biology to know that the muscles from the edges of my mouth and up around my ears are connected directly to chemical responses in my brain. I knew that if I held that smile long enough, some natural chemicals—endorphins, dopamine, and serotonin—would be forced into my brain. The endorphins act as a little bit of pain reliever, the serotonin is the brain's natural antidepressant, and the dopamine would give me some small level of joy. Even the slightest joy—I needed that right then. I did not want to smile. Nothing in me wanted to smile, but I forced it there and held it. To a passerby, that smile would have probably looked more like a grimace, but I knew that wouldn't matter to my brain. The chemicals would flow anyway because of the muscle contractions.

I felt those little tears on my cheeks as I forced that smile and held my eyes closed. I wiped them away and continued to smile. I took deep breaths, purposefully slowing them down even further. Finally, there it was—that calm that I knew as the truth, my truth. My heart had slowed, and the smile was more natural and less of a grimace now as I continued to hold it. More and more, with the proper brain chemicals sloshing around in the little bit of gray matter I possess, I could relax and even eventually began to chuckle a little. Slowly I started to feel bad for her. My reasoning and my logic started to return to me. My learning was still there. I felt pity for her. I saw her face again in my mind's eye as she said those words, "Well, if it's in the book," and

I took control. I decided what I wanted to feel. I made the decision about how I would feel. I didn't just step back into an old knee-jerk emotional habit. I knew the choice about how I wanted to feel was really up to me. I knew I could choose, and so I did choose. I took responsibility for what I could do. I couldn't love her in that moment. Nope. Love was not within my power just yet, but I could still choose to feel gratitude for the love she had shown me as a very young man. I could still choose to feel gratitude that I now know better and I know a lot more than the young man that she thought she was talking to... "mhm-mhm." I clung to that gratitude and allowed her to possess the ignorance to which she was clinging. Her spiritual growth was not my responsibility. It was not my job to change her. That job belonged to someone else—her. My job was to forgive her. Breathing and smiling is where I began.

I was visiting my mom in my hometown, actually the town twelve miles down the road from my hometown. It was the town I was bussed into for school—I'm a country kid, ya'll. I had rarely stepped back in that town during the last forty years. In a very natural and healthy way, I still feel an affection for the sweet people during that part of my life and the good memories I have of them. As difficult as many things were in my childhood, there were good times. There were so many people that I thought would be fun to see, but only for a casual moment, a chance encounter. I honestly didn't know how most of these people felt about me, a gay man who had left this rural Southern town so many years ago. But I kept telling myself that people change and people grow just like I have. It would be fun if I could just run into these people in an unexpected and unplanned way. Where could that happen in a natural way? Where do people gather? Of course... church! Yes, I naively thought that was a great idea. So I went.

19

This church was not the church of my early childhood, what we call a "home church," but it was a church I attended a lot in my senior year of high school because I wanted to be with the other kids my age. And it did have special meaning to me because it represented the age of decision. It wasn't the church my parents took me to; it was a church that I chose to attend when I had the maturity to drive and choose for myself.

I got to the church and asked some faces I didn't recognize where I could sit close to the Browns (not their real name). I was told that both of them had special duties that morning, so they wouldn't be sitting in the congregation, but they pointed out where they normally sat. So that's where I went and sat down. They asked who I was so they could tell the Browns I was there, so I told them my name.

This is not a large church. There were maybe a hundred people in attendance. And it being a small country town, visitors are not frequent. People were looking back at me, the stranger, and then I saw it happening. I saw the familiar whisper followed by the nodding of the heads and the mouth shape of "oh." It was obvious that news was spreading around the church that I was there. Remember, I grew up here, and they haven't seen me as a sixty-year-old man with gray hair and a beard.

The service began, and then the preacher stepped up to the pulpit and began his sermon. Much to my surprise, the preacher started to rant and despair over the sins of homosexuality. Now mind you, this church is full of divorced people caught in affairs, gossipers, slanderers, and obese people, and some in attendance could even be called "insolent, arrogant, and boastful." But when it came to the long list of perceived sins in Romans 1, all the preacher wanted to talk about this morning was homosexuality. I was not going to let him get to me; I just glazed over my heart. I knew how to do this. I had done enough personal work that a simple sermon by a preacher that I had never met, a man I didn't know, was not going to get to me. It was so obvious it was almost a joke to me. So I sat through it with my heart glazed over in protection. I even stayed for the offertory, and no, I didn't put a dime in that plate.

By the time the service ended, I had realized all this was a bad idea. I knew it had ended up being a great laugh at my expense and fodder for the righteous, but I really didn't care. As I was slipping out the front doors of the church, I saw Mrs. Brown. I smiled at her and hung my head a little. I knew she would feel compassion. I said, "I can't imagine homosexuality is such a big topic normally in this church, so I guess that sermon was directed straight at me." As she turned on her heel to begin to walk away from me, she said over her shoulder, "Well, if it's in the book." And then that slight giggle.

When I got to my car, I had to make a choice. The sermon had barely made a dent in my psyche, but this woman, in one sentence, had knocked me to my knees. I had the choice to go immediately into an age-old habit of remaining in that fear and pain, or I could use the tools that I knew I had at my disposal. I didn't want to use the tools. I wanted to just spiral out of control and swim in a deep pond of self-pity, but I chose to use my tools. It was hard. I was in pain, but I chose.

Good medicine doesn't mean anything to someone who is sick if they can't take it. Knowing, learning, and practicing tools designed to help you stay stable in a moment of despair have no value if you aren't willing to use them. Taking all the classes in the world is great, but if you refuse to use what you learn, it's pointless. If I had grown up to be a model Christian and had something similar happen to me, I might have been able to go back to my car, close my eyes, and say, "Lord... I come to you now and ask you to forgive Mrs. Brown for the pain she has just put in my heart. I know she didn't mean to hurt me, Lord, and I am so grateful that you have given me the strength to not punch that old battle-ax right in the mouth, Lord." However, I was never that good of a Christian. I needed something far beyond what I had been taught as prayer because that prayer... was not going to cross my lips, much less pour out of my heart. And it certainly wasn't going to take away the fear I felt in that moment.

Again, just knowing something exists isn't worth a hill of beans until you can actually use it. For me to gain control of myself and to change my thoughts and beliefs, I had to do more than just know about other theologies in the world. I had to do more than just *know* there was a morality system other than the Evangelical equation of birth + life + death = heaven or hell. I had to, as Paul says, work out my salvation daily... but I was sick of the "fear and trembling" part. I had to actually choose to find out about other theologies that were joyful and to be open-minded enough to implement some of those things into my life. Being open-minded is a very scary thing for someone raised as a fundamentalist because we are all taught fear and loathing from a very young age.

As a child, I was taught that there is life after death, and when you die, one of two things happens—heaven or hell. You either go to heaven and walk the streets of gold, sing with the angels, and be in the presence of God, or you go to hell and live in fiery torment for eternity, remain always in unimaginable pain, and your only company would be Satan himself. And, as a child, I kept thinking because of the heat and the fire, I was always going to be thirsty. Bad thirsty. Always. Very, very thirsty. Just being open-minded meant I was probably walking away from heaven and descending a slow stairway to hell. If it wasn't definite, it would, at the very least, make it a gamble tilted toward losing. I was taught that life after death was simple. You could either know for certain you were going to heaven, or it was, at best, a toss of weighted dice that you would probably be going to hell.

You weren't even allowed to simply not go to church without being considered a backslider. When you die as a backslider, you will still be saved by grace, but at best, you might end up in a little shack on the back forty acres of heaven. You might be able to walk up and enjoy the streets of gold, but you're not going to be living on one. Just being a backslider might be good enough for some people who are dissatisfied with fundamentalism. And maybe their sins didn't seem as heavy to them as the one I was born with, but it just wasn't good enough for me. I still believed in truth and honesty, and I knew I had to find a way to live truthfully and honestly. It took a long time, but I finally found enough inclusive theology in this world to form a new idea of what the word *God* meant to me, and I have never felt so alive.

With the way I live today and the freedom I feel in life, I get a kick out of the responses I get when people ask me what I do for a living, and I tell them I'm a hypnotist. Hypnosis has been around for a very long time, and yet the resistance from some people that's based upon misinformation or superstition is astonishing. Let me give you a sample of responses:

"Oh... everyone, quick, put your hands on your wallets."

"Oh, I'm too afraid of losing control to do hypnosis."

"Ha! I was told I'm one of those people who is too strong-minded to be hypnotized."

"So, can you make me hate eating sweets?"

"Can you hypnotize my wife to love me again?"

"I'm afraid if I went into a trance, I wouldn't be able to come out again."

"I don't take suggestions very well."

"Do you also read palms?"

"I heard that was of the Devil."

Hypnosis has been in and out of popularity since the 1700s. Yes, it's been around that long. It was first developed by medical doctors to help with surgeries before chemical anesthesia was invented. Just by using hypnosis, the doctors upped their survival rate of amputation by fifty percent. And yet, as long as it has been around, in many cultures, it still exists only on the fringes of society and is looked at with skepticism. Over the years, I've learned to listen to people. And when you listen, they will tell you exactly who they are.

"Oh... everyone, quick, put your hands on your wallets."

As much as this is intended as a joke, it communicates a clear level of distrust. This person feels easily tricked. They might even be someone who is willing to deceive others because they know they are easily deceived. Usually, this person only knows hypnosis from television, movies, or a hypnosis show. (Oh, and I love a good hypnosis show. I'd like to do one someday.)

"Oh, I'm too afraid of losing control to do hypnosis."

This person already feels somewhat out of control. What they don't understand is that hypnosis is not about losing control. In fact, it's just the opposite; it gives you control. Submitting to a habit, whether it's physical or emotional, is being out of control. Hypnosis allows you choice. That's real control.

"Ha! I was told I'm one of those people who is too strong-minded to be hypnotized."

Well, it might seem clear to you that this statement is full of both fear and insecurity. It is a clear expression of being afraid of being made a fool or taken advantage of. "I'm too smart for that." When I encounter someone like this, I make sure they understand that I already see them as smart.

"So, can you make me hate eating sweets?"

No. And in truth, you wouldn't want me to do that because there's a level of subtle sweetness in most foods, which is why we continue to eat them. Think of the nuanced and natural sweetness in corn, green beans, rice, and especially fruit. You wouldn't want to miss out on those things! But even more importantly, hypnosis is not about making anyone do anything. There's a lot of fun in a hypnosis show on stage, but not in hypnosis for change, and especially in self-hypnosis. This person feels powerless. I help them understand that hypnosis can help them understand the power they already possess but don't always use.

"Can you hypnotize my wife to love me again?"

Again, no. This guy has already pushed my *unlikeable* button. I'd probably just leave it at that. He clearly can't take responsibility for his own actions and behavior. It doesn't cross his mind that the problem could be him, and he certainly isn't willing to alter his behavior to become more lovable.

"I'm afraid if I went into a trance, I wouldn't be able to come out again."

This person has a big misconception about what hypnosis is. When I explain the many times a day that people naturally go into a hypnotic trance and give them examples, they understand better. I help them understand that you are even more alert and aware when you are purposely using hypnosis than when you are not. Then I'll make a joke about taking some drugs you bought off the street. Now that can get you stuck! And they laugh.

"I don't take suggestions very well."

Sometimes I will say, "I know a lot of people like that." This person is often married to the guy who wants me to hypnotize his wife to love him again! Sometimes, while I'm talking with them, I pretend to see something on their cheek, and finally, they will reach up and touch their face. Then I'll give a knowing smile, and usually, they get it and laugh.

"Oh, do you also read palms?"

This response tells me they have an association with hypnosis and the occult, and they are either afraid or they really like it. Either way, it is a wrong assumption that I can easily dispel with something as simple as "No, and I don't talk to dead people either."

"I heard that was of the Devil."

This is obviously a very strong, fear-based response that comes from a fundamental theological system that usually contains a lot of superstition. This person needs the Devil. In their mind, there is always some satanic and evil force at play in the world, tripping them up. One of the biggest challenges with this person is they have a hard time recognizing a consequence as simply the result of a bad choice. I would call this *Eve Syndrome,* but it's not just women who have it.

This is only a handful of the funny responses I get. But combining all the above characteristics into one person—distrust, feeling out of control, fear of being taken advantage of or being made to look foolish, feeling powerless, unwilling to look at what makes them unlovable, being stuck in life, unwilling to consider the good advice of others, making everything be about the occult, living within a world of superstition based upon a fear of someone or something different that you call "the other"—creates an interesting but troubled person. I also realize it's a perfect description for many people I know. How about you? Do you recognize anyone in that description?

I just described a person stuck in emotional patterns, and by thinking them over and over, the patterns have become emotional habits. Where is the freedom of personal choice when all you feel is distrust of other people? If you no longer have a cognitive choice, it's a habit. I am also familiar with that feeling of being out of control, and I know how horrible and destructive it is when you are trying to live a deeper and more meaningful life.

I have never felt any sense of empowerment while I was feeling stuck in an emotional habit, and yes, there were many times when I refused to listen to the good advice of others. Have you done that? It took me decades to be able to un-believe the fundamentalist theology I was taught as a child and utilize the life experiences of the other people living around me. What a great benefit we all would have if we could trust the freedom of being able to talk openly and curiously about spiritual principles that bring meaning to other cultures. But that is impossible within the dogmatic clothing of most religions. In fear, they only want to hear the dogma that is their own. What sense of deep spiritual connection with the world around you is possible when you have been indoctrinated to avoid the other at all costs? I remember clearly there was no real peace while living in fear that the devil might be in control of my neighbor around the very next corner. Or in control of me.

Polls continue to prove that people in this century are leaving the traditional church in large numbers. In March 2021, *Gallup News* reported that U.S. church membership had fallen below a majority of citizenship for the first time. Church membership in the U.S. was at 73 percent when Gallup first started measuring it in 1937. It remained near 70 percent for the next 60 years. But in 2020, church membership had declined to only 47 percent of adult citizens. At the same time, Pew Research tells us that the phrase "spiritual but not religious" has become more and more popular among Americans as a way to describe their belief identity. Back in the day, I would have called "spiritual but not religious" a pretty fancy definition of a backslider. But today, I see real spiritual struggle represented by these numbers. It's a struggle to open up and find something different theologically. People want something inclusive and loving, and that is why I am writing this book and sharing this information with you. The truths I bring to this book have set me free and given me a sense of freedom I never felt empowered to feel within traditional church dogma. I know you can experience this same power, peace, and sense of joy that is you. It's written here in these pages for you to see with your eyes, feel in your heart, and imagine in your open mind.

Chapter 3

Important Questions

I am often asked:

- Do you still believe in God?
- Do you still believe in the Bible?
- Do you still believe in life after death?
- Do you believe in reincarnation?
- Isn't this just repackaged humanism?
- Doesn't this really just make you an atheist?

At this point in my life, I don't feel any need to apologize or defend what I believe. So in real-time face-to-face conversations, I don't usually pay too much attention to these types of questions. But since this is not real-time, and you don't know me as a person, and you can't see the sincerity in my face (that I'm told I manage to mix with a twinkle of mischief), let me briefly tackle each of these.

Do you still believe in God?

Yes, I absolutely believe in God. What I do not believe is the concept of God that I was taught as a child. I believe in an infinite something that is much greater than the confines of any book or story. This entire book is filled with what I believe God to be, so keep reading.

Do you still believe in the Bible?

In the Bible? No, I am not an idol worshipper. I do not believe *in* the Bible. I do not give the Bible any magical power that would make it infallible. Posturing the Bible in this manner gives it equal status to God and therefore makes it an idol. I believe the Bible is a wonderful and treasured resource of wisdom. It is a collection of books, a library of beliefs about God from a specific set of people—actually two sets of people at specific times in their histories. I love the Bible. I love it so much that I do not worship it.

Do you still believe in life after death?

I believe in the eternality of energy. I am energy. Since I believe I am energy and the scientific law of energy tells me that energy can neither be created nor destroyed—only converted from one form to another—I believe my energy cannot be destroyed, simply converted. Nor can it be created, simply converted. What does that mean for my personal consciousness? This is where choice comes in because I do not know. I can also listen to the life experiences of others and add those stories to my choices. And so I choose to believe in the continuance of a collection of energy that I call "me." I have no evidence of this continuance beyond my own experience and the experiences of others who also believe the same as me. It is a belief that I choose, and I am fine with that.

Do you believe in reincarnation?

31

I don't know. I can see why some people do, and I can see why some people don't. I was recently watching a video of a youngster only two years old being held up to a piano. This child was obviously making choices about notes, triad chords, hand positions, and chord progressions that it would have been impossible to teach. That child just knew. It was as if they had a lifetime of experience already playing that instrument. So I don't know. What I do believe is that it doesn't matter. I'm focused on this life and not one before or after what I am conscious of living now.

Isn't this just repackaged humanism?

Well, I don't think so. I guess that depends on how you define humanism and the source of your definition. For me, this is humanistic because it comes from the human experience but not humanism because I'm still pushing the boundaries of my own personal awareness further into the eternal Consciousness that I call God. I'm not taking God out of the equation; I'm putting God in the center of the equation instead of "way out there somewhere." For me, there is no path to God. You are the path, and I am the path because we are each the expression of God.

Doesn't this just really make you an atheist?

Again, no. Just because I don't define God in the triad or believe in a salvation-based theology, and just because I do define God in more scientific terms than traditional Christianity, doesn't mean I don't believe in a God at all. And since I do believe in God, I cannot be considered an atheist. Although, I really like a lot of them.

I experience God in me, around me, and as me. I am absolutely certain that when you begin to see God in this same way instead of away from you and something far in the distance that you have to find your way back to—a path to—you will realize a life for yourself that is also more powerful, more satisfying, and more peaceful. But it is still always going to come down to you and your willingness to use what you learn. Some of the ideas I bring into this book might at first seem odd to you or maybe even disrespectful, and that is where your open mind will become essential. You can't grasp a new idea while your hands are still full of the old one. You have to be willing to temporarily set something down in order to pick something else up. Don't worry. Anything you set down will still be waiting for you if you decide you still need it.

1. What is God?

Well, isn't that a challenging subject? When talking about God, we generally talk about who God is and what God has done, but I rarely hear anyone talk about what God is. I think this might be emotionally the most difficult topic of all for people to come to grips with. Christians have read or heard someone say, "God created us in His image," with such redundancy that they have a hard time not also reversing the statement and creating God in their image. It's easier to understand and love a God that looks like you and has your values even when He doesn't give you what you want.

2. The Brain

Oh, this magnificent collection of matter, nerves, neurons, chemicals, and a smattering of magic that we call the brain. It controls so much of our lives and how we perceive the world around us. And to think that we actually have control over how we shape it! We actually shape the functions of our brains through our everyday living, our speech, and our emotional patterns. Why does no one teach us this?

3. Consciousness

What exactly is consciousness? Is it simply our awareness, or is it something much more? How does my consciousness affect my everyday life, and what kind of theological ideas should I have about my own existence and the fact that I am aware that I exist?

4. Quantum

Oh no! This can't be a spiritual discussion if you insist on using scary science words! Well, you are not alone in that feeling! But when I allow myself to feel a little stupid, I can actually enjoy reading about things that I don't fully understand. And even better, what makes this particular science so intriguing is that no one completely agrees on what any of it means, even the scientists! This is what Albert Einstein referred to as "spooky action at a distance." Here's the great thing: We don't have to understand it to use it! Do you understand electricity? I know some of you do, but most of us don't. And yet we aren't afraid to flip on a light switch!

5. Hypnosis

Hypnosis has been around for centuries, and yet so many people have so many misconceptions about what hypnosis is. During certain patches of history, hypnosis was even relegated to witchcraft. You might be surprised to learn how natural hypnosis is to the human brain and how often you use it in a very natural way every single day.

6. Hypnotic Techniques Already Used in the Church

Knowing that hypnosis is natural to the human brain and that there are many things we do that are naturally hypnotic in nature, of course, it's going to be found in human ceremonies. Many rituals become hypnotic in nature because of their repetition. Worship services in all religious denominations have tremendous amounts of repetition, and those participating slide very naturally right into a hypnotic state. I'll give you some examples, and when you know what you are seeing, you will know what you are seeing!

7. Similarities between Hypnosis and Prayer

What if I told you they were the same thing? What if prayer is actually just hypnosis interpreted out of a specific religious culture? What if hypnosis is actually just prayer interpreted out of a specific religious culture? Is prayer more than just spiritual? Is it also physiological? Well, that is a great question. If it's happening in the body—the thought process through the brain—then it has to be physiological. People were praying long before the study of hypnosis came into being, but that doesn't mean prayer and hypnosis are different. That just means we started to understand it on a scientific level. What if using the applied techniques of hypnosis in prayer could make it stronger and lift it out of only a sense of hope?

8. How Do We Use It?

Well, isn't that the reason you came to this book? And yes, I will finally get to some of the techniques that can be implemented in your life.

Let me restate again. I am a man of faith. I believe in God. I just don't believe in the concept of God that I was handed as a child. I have lived an interesting, beautiful, sometimes really hard, gorgeous life that has had an abundance of diversity and experience. I have used that diversity to add to my faith and grow my spiritual heart. I enjoy the freedom to be able to sit with people of many faiths, to trust in their spirit, and not feel any need to convert them to my brand of faith. My God is not branded. My God is everyone's God and is at the core of all of life, all of creation.

Hypnosis allows me to pray without ever needing to bow before God because, for me, God is an assumption. Everything dwells within God. I dwell within God. God in me as me is me. There is no path to God. My path to God is me. I never have to beg God or ask permission from God, or say, "but... thy will be done." But? Where is the faith in "but"? "Thy will be done," is a given to me because I don't believe God is a distant being that is separate from me and hanging out somewhere in the distance, granting wishes. And I don't feel a need to blame God's will on my failure to create the change in my life that I desire. I am responsible for my life, how I respond to it, and how I create it.

So just keep reading. There may be points in this book where you question me and the way I think. I don't mind. I really don't. Just keep reading. Give yourself a chance to think something different for only a minute. Let yourself question what you have been taught. It is in questioning that faith deepens. Questioning will give you a stronger foundation of faith because you either find something new that satisfies you more or you return to your original belief with a stronger sense of knowing. I just know that if you pick up only a couple of things in this book, those new ideas will deepen your faith and create more happiness in your life, and you'll be glad you kept reading. So keep reading.

Chapter 4

God

I read a story recently about a young kindergarten teacher watching her classroom during art hour. She liked to walk around the room and see each child's intense face as they expressed their feelings with paper and crayons. Pictures of families, pets, and favorite vacation moments were often expressed by these children, and of course, the sun would be shining brightly in the corner of the page. This morning she came to one little girl who was working so diligently. The teacher asked her what she was drawing.

The little girl said, "I'm drawing God."

Taken aback, the teacher said, "But no one knows what God looks like."

And without the slightest hesitation, the little girl replied, "Well, they will in a minute."

Inconsistency is tricky. Have you ever noticed that? Do you have friends that are so inconsistent you just never know exactly who they are going to be? Do you call them on the phone and wonder which personality is going to answer? Is "helpful" Benji going to answer the phone, or will it be "mean" Benji? Will it be "compassionate" Benji or "bitchy" Benji? "Calm" or "anxious Benji?"

Inconsistency is confusing in a career setting too. In fact, inconsistency is always confusing in any type of relationship. So, of course, inconsistency is confusing when you're talking about God. Is this the "All-loving and compassionate" God, or the "Send me to hell because I am a sinner" God? Is this the "Pray to me when you want something, and you will have it if you pray believing your prayer will be answered" God, or is it the "But thy will be done" God? Who are we talking about? And even more importantly, what are we talking about?

When I ask people the question, "What is God?" they usually seem stumped. Typically they'll stutter and nervously begin spouting off the most common answers they learned as a child in church:

- "God created the heavens and the earth. Oh, and us!"
- "God is our heavenly Father."
- "God is the head of the trinity: the Father, the Son, and the Holy Ghost."
- "God is the alpha and omega."
- "God is our creator and our savior."

All these answers give a peek into their personal beliefs about God, what God has done, or God's position within the spiritual realm. But none of these answers give the most basic answer to what God actually is. Most people can tell me something about what they believe about God, but they struggle to find words that express what they believe God to actually be.

What is God? What is God made of? Where is God? To what, not whom, but to what am I actually sending prayers? Without answers to these questions, how can anyone really expect an answer to prayer?

Infinity is big—no, I mean, really big. A complete comprehension of infinity is impossible because it is infinite. And so fully knowing God is also impossible because God is Infinity. But having reasonable, logical, and consistent answers to these questions will help create a more satisfying relationship with God when you are trying to create specific change in your daily life.

God is It

I was so uncomfortable the first time I read a description of God as simply "It." I was reading a book, *The Science of Mind*, written by Dr. Ernest Holmes, and the opening chapter is titled "The Thing Itself." I was eager to learn something new, but neither Thing nor It seemed holy enough to use in reference to God. As abused as I had been by fundamentalist doctrine, some of it was really hard to let go of. However, the more I read his book, the more I grew to see "Thing" and "It" as two of the most reverent and inclusive words I could possibly use when talking about God. I soon accepted that "It" was so much more inclusive, loving, and responsive to me than "He" had ever been. I really started to love It.

The Jewish, Christian, and Muslim faiths very distinctly give God a gender identity of male and the patriarchal position of Father. This is an ancient tradition that, for some, gives a warm undertone to the idea of God. It also

39

establishes a parent-child structure for prayer dialogue. Because of my own horrible relationship with my father, I always had a problem with the God-as-father relationship. But beyond simply projecting all my daddy issues on God, prescribing a gender identity to Infinity is completely illogical.

When looking for a cleaner definition of what God is, neither He nor She is in any way accurate because God is so completely both! I understand the desire to paint God as a loving parent because, at first, loving the coldness of Infinity is a real challenge. However, using human relationships as a structure for trying to understand Infinity and as a power that only operates for good also presents its own challenges because we project not only our strengths (love) onto God but also our weaknesses (wrath). Poor God. Beyond not being at all accurate, it simply isn't fair! We are constantly blaming God for our own shortcomings and calling it "God's will." With absolute reverence, I now prefer the cleanness of seeing God as the Thing or It. And you will see me capitalize those and other words that reference God, like Consciousness.

God is All

When we, as humans, create something, we use resources as building materials. To create a house, we use the wood of trees or bricks and stones. To create the chemicals used in modern medicine, we mix the primary elements found in earth. I'm a musician. I create music. But in order to create music, I use tones and build them into chords and melodies. Whatever we create, we do it by combining already existing resources to build new creations. I wonder... to create the galaxies of the Universe, what did God use as Its building material? What substance was the pre-matter resource of the Universe? Before creation, there was only God. There was nothing but Itself to use, and It created. God, using Its own substance as the pre-material building blocks, created all that is from Itself, within Itself. This is important to understand because if God is infinite, there can be no place set aside that is outside of God. To create the Universe, God had to create within Itself. If God is anything, It has to be infinite, or else it wouldn't be God. There is no place and no thing outside Infinity.

This simple logic leads me to a deeply profound realization. Suddenly... all that is becomes All-That-Is. God is All-That-Is. God is the material stuff of Earth, our Moon, and the Sun. God took Its own substance and shaped it into every planet, every star, and every galaxy in the night sky. God is the stuff of every rock, every tree, and every molecule forming every living thing. It created all the fish in the ocean, every bird in the air, the entire animal kingdom, the insect kingdom, and the plant kingdom. It created All-That-Is out of Its own Substance and within Its own Self.

The profundity of this theory is not limited to merely the scope of creation but expands my consciousness to a more complete realization that there can be nothing outside of God, for God is All. Mathematically and philosophically, I understand that being outside of All is an impossibility. You may feel I'm beating this point to death, but it's so important. God is All-That-Is. God is All-That-Will-Be. And in a time that was before time, It created All from Its Self. There has never been and never will be any place, thing, or person outside of God. God is All.

Understanding God as All is of utmost importance in prayer and in hypnosis because All is the medium in which we, as St. Luke said in Acts 17, "live and move and have our being." But since God is All, it is also how we are all connected. Yes, we must be connected because each of us is the one Thing. God as All is the freedom-giving realization that there is no pathway to God. Realizing this, you no longer have to search for a pathway to God. You are It. Any pathway or savior-based theology is founded upon separation: the idea that something can be outside of God or set aside. Naturally, this separation anxiety creates a strong survival urge to find a path back to where God is or to find a savior that will take you there. But if God created All-That-Is from Itself, as our most treasured traditions teach—Genesis 1, "In the beginning God created the heavens and the earth"—separation is an impossibility.

As a young man, my elders convinced me that I was lost. I cannot tell you the relief I received when I finally understood that I cannot be lost because there is no place in which to lose me. God is All, and "outside of God" does not exist. Being lost is a feeling, and it can be a very real feeling, but it is not a spiritual reality. There is only God, and we all have our entire life experience within It. When this life experience ends, there is no "outside of God" to send us to. God is All. The first time I understood that my entire psyche just went, "Whew. That's a fear I'm glad to be done with."

God is Intelligence

Everywhere I look, all of creation, and therefore all of God, displays order and intelligence. The stars, planets, and moons are ordered into solar systems and galaxies that are alive with movement. My cells, down to their most minute molecular structures, demonstrate intelligence. My infinitely complex body systems work seamlessly together, demonstrating the infinite Intelligence of God at work on a personal level. Plants and insects demonstrate intelligence, and their cell structure has intelligence. Even the molecular structure of rocks acts with intelligence holding the rocks together.

Within that Intelligence, I also see what appears to be chaos. However, chaos is ultimately creative. A deconstruction of anything leads to a reconstruction of something new. Stars in the Universe explode. Those exploding stars created all the elements we have here on Earth that generate life and sustain life. Our bodies are made up of the dust of exploded stars. Chaos becomes order. When we stop judging things by our human values as right and wrong, chaos leading to order makes sense. I know some of you are immediately thinking of the chaos of human disease and wondering what possible order comes out of that. Disease leads to death. I think the comfort or discomfort anyone feels with the chaos of disease has more to do with their beliefs and especially their feelings about their current life, and then add to those feelings what they believe about what happens in death. Those two sets of ideas and feelings may clash more than their simple agreement that chaos leads to order.

I love the night sky. It's one of the things I miss most about living in the desert. There are places in the desert that are so far away from light pollution that at night you can get a glimpse into Infinity as you gaze upon the Milky Way. I can stare into that deep black canvas and imagine the joyful glee that God might feel as It demonstrates only a fraction of Infinite-Intelligence through Its always-changing, physically manifested expression of Consciousness that we call Creation. God is the Intelligence in the design, beauty, and living function of All.

God is Good

Ernest Holmes used to have a radio program and he would open every program with the following: "There is a power for good in the Universe, greater than you are, and you can use it."

Pause a moment, and for greatest effect, restate that last sentence, and hear it in your head as a booming, old-school radio voice with maybe some organ music underneath. This was a wonderful thing for me to hear, and I know it is what so many people seek—a "power greater than you are." But as much as we want and would love that distant power to be usable by us, his opening statement places the "power for good" outside of ourselves. Over the years, I've come to adjust that statement just a bit. "There is a power for good in the Universe greater than your occasional use and awareness of It. You are It, and you can use It more, and you can use It better."

God is only good. God is pure good. God is perfect good. God is Good. Those statements seem really easy to agree upon, as long as you don't dig too deeply. But if you dig deeply, you are going to discover that if God is only good and God is infinite, then there is no Devil, no Satan, and evil is not an actual entity. There can be no Devil because he would have to have his existence within God. Remember, there is no such place as outside of God.

People really like Satan. They need him. Flip Wilson, a comedian in the 1970s, famously had a drag persona, Geraldine Jones. Geraldine always said, "The Devil made me do it." She needed the Devil because, without the Devil, she would have to take responsibility for what she said and did. Flip managed to make great comedy out of the human condition and the need for blame. Satan is a handy pal when it comes to blame. But that is not to say that evil does not exist. It does. However, what we experience as evil is actually a lack of good. We experience evil as an action, not an entity. Evil is not an entity in itself, just as darkness is not an entity. The experience of darkness is also very real, but darkness is just a lack of light. Darkness is not a thing. There isn't a ray of darkness, but there is a ray of light. And the experience of evil is also very real, but it is simply a lack of good. When light is introduced, darkness is gone. When good is introduced, evil also vanishes.

So what is God? God is All-That-Is, an infinite Intelligence that is backed by the unlimited energy of Creation. It is Infinite-Intelligence, and It is Good. Scientifically speaking, It is not only the particles of the atom, but It is also the space between the particles. It is my every breath. It is Consciousness.

I started this chapter by telling a story about a little girl drawing a picture of God. I sure wish I could see that picture.

Chapter 5

Consciousness

How do you pray for yourself and try to create change in yourself if you don't really know what your "self" is? What is my "self?" What is this awareness inside my body that inhabits my body that I also recognize is not my body and that I realize I am? Wait... I am? Did I just make a statement of self-realization or an Old Testament name of God reference? And are they the same thing?

I can only do it for very brief periods. I'm not sure how long exactly—a millisecond to a couple of seconds. And then I'll do it again for several more. I don't realize I'm doing it until I've stopped doing it; then I recognize I was doing it, and I'm waiting to do it again. I've done it in the city, but it happens easiest if I'm in nature. I've done it sitting alone in a wooded forest, on a deserted ocean beach, and also by a running creek. I do it best when I focus on something in nature and something that has a distinct sound only found in nature. But it can also sometimes happen just from the sun shining really brightly on my face when I have my eyes closed. And although it's not as easy, I've done it with my eyes open.

I've experimented with this many times and found it's easiest when I'm warm and comfortable, and the temperature is at that perfect point where my skin is at its least sensitive. I'll clasp my hands together or put my hands on something that doesn't give my fingertips any type of sensation that would distract me. I'll adjust my sitting position until I'm completely comfortable and then close my eyes. After a couple of deep breaths, I'll start to breathe very lightly; breaths so shallow it's almost like not breathing. I'll close my eyes and then begin to listen. I only listen. I'm not searching for sounds. Instead, I'll fall into the sounds of what's around me. And because of my environment, usually somewhere alone in nature, what I hear is not man-made. Music won't work for me because it's human expression, not Consciousness expressing. I'm a musician, so music just pulls at my attention and begs me to analyze what I'm hearing. That's the opposite of what I'm attempting to do. I'm trying to release everything. So I sit and listen to nature and what is not human: the birds, the creek, the waves, the air, the dog in the distance, a squirrel barking—Consciousness expressing. Releasing any effort, I relax into those sounds and let them come to me. I reduce all my attention to that one sensory preceptor—the auditory. The sound of continued creation is what I sit and wait for as I listen. And while I'm waiting, it happens. I will suddenly realize that for a brief second, I had done it; I was gone. My body was gone. I had left behind most of my attachment to my body and my identity as human, and in that focused moment of pure observation, I had become as close to pure consciousness as any other way I have experienced. After it happens, I try not to move. I simply listen again and know I will do it repeatedly, but only for very brief periods. I won't know I'm doing it until it has already happened and stopped. Then I realize I'm individuated again; I'm aware of my selfness. And I'm waiting... again.

I've had hunters describe this same experience as they are sitting on a deer stand waiting for that moment when the deer steps out into the open. I've also had people who fish describe this sensation where they stare at the water so long that they feel like they are one with the water, the lake.

Consciousness

Language frequently fails us in its limitations. There are multiple overlapping yet slightly different definitions for important words. "Love" is one of those words. If you say you love someone, you might mean loving them like a parent, which is different from loving them like a friend. And both of those are very different from loving someone as a lover. *Consciousness* is also one of those words. *Consciousness* may be a reference to whether a person's body is responsive enough that they are awake and responsive, "Are they conscious?" On the other hand, it could also be asking if someone has direct knowledge of some specific fact or action, "Did they do it consciously?" And, of course, it can also be a reference to a person who closes their eyes and becomes acutely aware of their own individuated self-awareness. All these definitions are in some way connected to the human brain. But does consciousness come out of a functioning brain, or does the function of the brain arise within consciousness? That sounds very similar to the chicken and egg question, doesn't it? It's also a question that has plagued scientists, theologians, and philosophers for millennia. Finally, I get to answer it for everyone!

In this chapter, I will talk about three aspects of individuated consciousness and how it interacts with the human brain. I'm going to present ideas about what we call the conscious mind, the unconscious mind, and the subconscious mind, as well as the functions of each. When I want to create change in my life, I find it helpful to know what aspect of me and my mind needs adjustment.

To keep it simple, most psychologists, psychiatrists, and hypnotists only divide the human mind into two categories: the conscious and then either the unconscious or subconscious, which are usually used interchangeably. Although the unconscious and subconscious function much the same way, there is a good argument for recognizing some difference between the two; but in truth, all of it is metaphorical, and the metaphors only help us to create categories for better understanding.

During our evolution, different parts of the brain evolved at different times, which gave us different brain organs, all with their own particular functions. The oldest parts of the brain are what I would call the subconscious mind. This regulates things like breathing, heart rate, and other bodily functions related to survival. That same area is also in control of the fight-or-flight chemicals in the brain. Those parts of the brain developed at a different time from what we could consider the more cognitive parts that control speech and give value and meaning to our experiences. Subconsciously, every cell in my body is communicating with the sum total of the rest of my body. These functions of the subconscious mind are not only automatic and outside my conscious thinking, but they are also below (sub) my ability to access them. It would be impossible for me to try to consciously regulate my bodily functions while also deciphering all the sensory triggers I'm receiving through my nervous system every second of every day; meanwhile, also feeling a great sense of urgency to apply value and significance to everything I encounter—at the same time, never ceasing to memorize all the sensory indicators associated with a specific encounter, so they can be triggered again in the future to let me interpret whether I'm in danger or supposed to be relaxed. Whew! Yes, that convoluted sentence was written on purpose and in that way to prove a point. We can all be grateful for the automatic and sub-level working of the subconscious mind. It's no wonder it needs a rest every night!

The unconscious mind is similar in that it's automatic, but much of the action, response, values, meaning, and triggers were filtered first through the conscious mind and then relegated to an unconscious and automated response. This happens for many reasons, the most common being repression or repetition and sometimes both. Unconscious mental activity is usually attached to some kind of trigger. It can be a sensory or emotional trigger. But regardless, when the trigger is activated, the unconscious response happens automatically without a conscious decision.

I have known many smokers who have a certain stoplight that acts as a trigger for them to smoke. It's that long one that just never seems to hit at the right time to be able to drive on through. And because it's a long light and they know they're going to be sitting there for several minutes, they automatically reach for the cigarette and light it up. They do not go through any thought process, making this a conscious choice: "Gee, would now be a good time for a cigarette? Do I really want one right now? Is this a good time? Yeah, I think I have plenty of time to get it out of my

50

purse, pocket, glove box, or from above the sunshade and light it up." That thinking and decision process just doesn't happen. They hit the light, grab one, and light up without even thinking about it. In their unconscious mind, it's all grouped together as one thing. The trigger is the stoplight, and smoking becomes an unconscious action.

I've known emotional eaters who have a trigger, and they'll reach for that snack of choice without even thinking about it. It doesn't matter who or what the trigger is. It might be the boss, family, husband, wife, kids, mother-in-law—you name it. But when the trigger has been pulled, they snack. They don't even have to enjoy what they're eating. They're fulfilling an action that's been set in motion by a trigger.

Emotional habits have triggers in the same way physical habits do. There may be a person from your past whose mere mention changes your mood. When you hear their name, you don't consciously make the choice: "Yeah, I think I'll sit here and be pissed off for a while. I think I'll take the next few minutes to remember what they did to me in every detail." No, that never happens. The unconscious mind has made it all much easier. Their name has become a trigger that will immediately and automatically change your mood. The trigger can also be something so subtle that you aren't even aware of it. For instance, you might suddenly smell something associated with that person, like a perfume or cologne. You may not even realize you smelled it, but it still produces a change in your mood, and you don't even realize why.

I don't want you to think I'm bashing the unconscious as all bad. Quite the contrary. Real estate agents use the smell of cookies at an open house to trigger feelings of happiness and home. When I was a child, we would pull down the Santa Claus pillow from the top of the storage closet. I would bury my face in that dusty pillow. To this day, the smell of a dusty pillow reminds me of Christmas.

The unconscious is also really useful in developing skills. I'm a musician. I sing, and I play the piano. And many times, I sing and play at the same time. When I sing and play simultaneously, one of these talents has to go into much more of an unconscious and automatic mental activity than the other. For me, that's the piano part, specifically the movement of my hands. I practice the singing and playing separately, and when I put them together, my hands go on automatic.

I know many dancers who will do the same thing. They know the movements of the dance, but there are triggers in the music that lead them from one movement to another. I was a singer in one of the last big Las Vegas spectaculars. I had this big production number with all the showgirls. During the song, I was spotlighted high up on a ladder at center stage, singing down to the showgirls while they performed a choreographed dance around me. All their dance moves and stage positioning had been choreographed specifically to the lyrics of my song. This one night, I made my way up that tall ladder, and to my dismay, I couldn't think of a single lyric to the song. Creatively, and with my conscious mind, I just started making up rhymes out of thin air. The words I chose had nothing to do with the song or each other—they just happened to rhyme. I created a mess on the stage. The fifteen beautifully costumed, topless showgirls began aimlessly walking around the stage to a bunch of rhyming gibberish flowing from my lips—all this in front of an audience of a thousand people. By the end of the number, the girls were nearly howling with laughter as that seemingly eternal song of rhyming nonsense finally ended. They never let me forget that performance.

I was making conscious-mind choices of rhyming words, and I stole their unconscious triggers for movement. At the chorus of the song, when I was out of rhymes and had given over to simply singing, "Oh, baby, baby. Can you hear me, baby, baby?" one of the girls was even bold enough to dance by my center stage ladder, look up and say, "Yes, baby, we can hear you."

Everything I've been discussing so far in this chapter about human consciousness is brain-related because it has all been activity related. I have talked about bodily functions like cell communication, heart rates, and breathing. I've talked about emotional habits that have physical triggers. I've even talked about physical activity that becomes unconscious because of repetition and familiarity. But there is also a greater aspect to consciousness that has to do with value and meaning. There is an unspoken meaning behind your unconscious activity. It has a value attached that gives it power. Value and meaning are not created in the brain. Value and meaning are found in the same place you discover inspiration and brilliance. Your brain is a computing machine that operates and interprets information into activity but not meaning. So where does meaning and value reside? And since we're asking, where is your mind located? Can you change your mind?

I'll dive deeper into all that in the next chapter, but before we go there, I want to remind you of my definition of what God is. There is only one Thing, and that is God. It is infinite in nature. There is no outside of God. And so my body, my brain, and also my mind are within God. We are all the same thing; therefore, we are all connected. I am hyper-aware of the experiential distinction between my body and

53

yours, my brain and yours. But my mind is not located in my body. So how do I know there is a separate distinction between my mind and yours? What if there is only one Mind, and we are all using It?

Chapter 6

Quantum Consciousness

I didn't care how it happened; I just wanted it to happen. So every few days, when it crossed my mind, I would close my eyes, take a few deep breaths, and then breathe shallowly. Next, I'd start to feel. I would create the feeling of how I wanted to feel, and when I felt that way, I became grateful.

I was floating on a tin can (cruise ship) in the middle of the Mediterranean Sea. I was fulfilling my final contract as a cruise ship entertainer. This had been a great career, and I felt fortunate to have seen far more of the globe than I had ever dreamed possible. But I was ready for a different experience in life, new challenges (like writing a book), and a new sense of belonging in this world. When I got on the ship for that last time, I listed my house for sale, and it sold quickly. I had decided to move across the country to be closer to family.

Once the house was sold, the fear of life after the tin became very real because I had no place to live. I had family very willing to provide me with a bedroom for a short while, but I didn't want to be a burden on them. It was a bit daunting to realize I wasn't going back to what I had called "home" for twenty years: all the old friends, familiar streets, and a favorite breakfast spot. Everything was going to be new to me. My new life was a reality, and it was all very exciting and all very scary at the same time.

I knew it was quite normal that all the unknowns in my new life would present themselves together and be a little scary and overwhelming. But thankfully, I had tools to work through all that scariness. I had mental exercises prepared to keep my anxiety at bay, and I didn't need a special place or a special time for the exercises. I didn't need to sit cross-legged with burning incense or chant "om." When I felt the slightest anxiety about the move, regardless of wherever I was, I could calm myself by doing the following:

- Acknowledge what I was feeling as fear, not based on any real danger.
- Ask myself what I would rather feel instead of what I was feeling.
- Knowing my fear was not based on any present danger, I set it aside and consciously created a new feeling of what I wanted to feel.
- Be grateful for the new feeling.

I would use a couple of breaths to stop the anxiety. For my new house that I did not yet have, I wanted to walk in and for it to feel homey, cozy, and comfortable. So I would imagine being there and having those feelings. I would consciously create within myself, my gut, a feeling of what I wanted my new home to feel like. I got very specific with the feelings. How did I want to feel when I sat in my big comfy chair watching television? How did I want to feel in my bedroom? How did I want to feel in my kitchen while I was cooking food? How did I want to feel having new friends to cook for? I didn't attach any visuals or specifics to the feelings. I didn't picture a house with a specific square footage or a specific neighborhood. In fact, I didn't try to visualize it in any way other than to feel it. It was important to think about how I would feel right then, in that moment, if I knew I were going home to the life that made me feel those feelings that I wanted to feel. I certainly wouldn't be feeling anxious. I would be grateful.

When I got the feeling I wanted, I switched my emotion to gratitude for the new feeling. Instead of only clinging to the feeling I had just created, I emoted gratitude for the new feeling. I let my body respond with emotion. Was I just pretending? Maybe but I think it was more. I prefer the word *imagining*. I was imagining that I already had the home that would generate those feelings, and imagining the feelings of being in that home allowed me to be grateful for it. In Mark 11, Jesus tells his disciples to pray, believing *it* has already been given to you. Gratitude is the key because you are never grateful for something you are longing for. You can only be grateful for what you already possess. After I felt what I wanted to feel in my new home, it was important to become grateful.

In the last chapter, I ended with some difficult questions about the mind. What is it? Where is it? Can you change your mind? What if there is only one mind, and we are all using it?

To begin to answer those questions, I will add one more level of consciousness to what we have already discussed, and it's going to be at the top of that list. In the last chapter, we discussed the conscious mind, the unconscious mind, and the subconscious mind. Now, let's talk about Quantum Consciousness or the Quantum Mind. As a hint, you might notice I capitalized it.

We live in a world of physics. And our physics world has scientifically proven laws by which it operates, or at least mostly. So my question is: What set the laws of physics into motion? It seems they sprung into action out of the chaotic hot mess that scientists call the Big Bang. But my Southern self asks, "But what sprung 'em?" What put these creative, intelligent, and organized laws of physics into motion? My answer: Consciousness. More specifically, Quantum Consciousness.

What is a quantum? A quantum is the smallest unit that something can be divided into. For example, a quantum of the United States dollar would be the penny. A quantum of light is a photon. A quantum of electricity is an electron. When you break matter down into its molecular components and then break those molecules into their particulates, there's still space between those particulates. What is the quantum of that space? There are all kinds of speculation about that, and the scientific term for it is "intermolecular space." The quantum metaphysics theorists also refer to it as Consciousness, Universal Consciousness, or, my favorite, Quantum Consciousness. In essence, it's the great swirling ocean of infinite Intelligence and infinite Energy in which all experiential matter exists.

Quantum physics provides the most sublime opportunities to look into our physical world and experience a profound spiritual connection. What if I told you that matter doesn't actually exist and that matter is not made up of anything real? Many quantum physicists tell us that everything we consider to be real is made up of particles that themselves are not actually real. If the particulates themselves are not real, then how can what they are assembled to create be real? It's impossible. According to many quantum scientists, there's no such thing as mass. The appearance and our experience of mass are only an energetic interaction between these massless phantom-like particles that make up molecules. That sounds crazy, right? But when you dig in deep, it all starts to make more sense. At least it does for a while, and then suddenly, you learn enough to realize that, actually, none of it makes any sense!

We have proven that subatomic objects don't actually exist as things, but instead, everything that exists is an interaction or a process. In his book *Quantum Revelation*, Paul Levy says, "The world is made up of a network of interactions. We cannot speak of the reality. Of a discrete entity outside the context of its range of interrelations with its environment. And other phenomena. Things forge their identity in relation to other things. Nothing stands alone." He goes on to say, "The only reality is the field in which all exists." The reality that he is talking about is Quantum Consciousness.

Science has come a long way from the Newtonian molecule models I saw in high school, which looked a lot like planetary orbits. We now know that electrons don't actually orbit the molecules' nucleus. Instead, molecules have an electron cloud of probabilities. And in that cloud, an electron can show up, disappear, and show up again somewhere else in a different place in the cloud without traveling between the two places. It can even leap from the probability cloud of its molecule over to another molecule, thus the term "quantum leap." Even more fun:

traditionally, we were taught that matter and waves are two different things, but it has been proven that when scientists break apart matter to its lowest degree (quantum), they have discovered that matter is actually just energy moving upon itself. More and more quantum physics is leading us in this direction of energy vs. matter.

There is a famous science experiment called the double-slit experiment. It was first produced in 1801, so this is not new science. Albert Einstein was fascinated by this subject and wrote about it at great length. The first time the double-slit experiment was done was in Britain by a scientist named Thomas Young. At that time, light was considered to be made up of quantum particles called photons. His experiment proved that light behaved as a wave and, therefore, was a wave, not tiny bits of matter. This was confusing to many scientists of the day, so over decades, they continued to do the experiment in different ways, and that's where it gets weird. They discovered that light behaved as either a wave or a particle, depending on what they were looking for.

Growth in scientific technology gave the opportunity for the double-slit experiment to be repeated with electrons instead of photons. These new experiments gave even more crazy outcomes because they discovered that an electron could actually be in two different places at once. Albert Einstein referred to some of these experiments as "Spooky action at a distance."

What determined whether the photon or the electron would show up as a particle or a wave? Just like the light photon, they would show up as whatever the scientists were looking for. This was referred to as the "observation effect." I'm presenting this in a very simplistic fashion, but basically, if they were looking for a wave, there it was. And when they were hoping for a particle, there it was. Crazy stuff. But exactly what is observing what? In order for the electron to show up as a particle or wave, it has to know it's being observed. In other words, the electron is observing the scientist observing it. Don't worry; the crazy just gets deeper and deeper the more you read about it. And there are any number of places where you can read about the double-slit experiment for more information. I'm not worried about the technical aspect of the experiment. I'm much more curious as to the implications, especially the effects of observation. Isn't observation the whole point of why most people pray? Aren't they attempting to find (observe) a particular condition in life changed and to experience a different outcome?

As you read this, your body is in a specific place and time. Most likely, your body is surrounded by clothing. If you are wearing cotton, it's composed of a combination of the elements: carbon, hydrogen, and oxygen. Each of these elements is made of molecules, and there's intermolecular space inside and between the molecules. In the center of the strand of cotton, the molecules are dense, and at the edge of the strand, they cling to the molecules leading toward the center. Some of those molecules from the edges of the strand of cotton touch your skin. Just like the cotton, the molecules of your skin are primarily composed of carbon, hydrogen, and oxygen. All these molecular particles in the cloth and in your skin have different combinations of the same ingredients and intermolecular space.

We've learned that the boundaries we experience in the physical realm do not actually exist in the quantum realm. This means that on a quantum level, there is no boundary between the cotton and your skin. We only experience a false boundary that's created by the nerve receptors in our skin that detect molecules vibrating at a different frequency, which is caused by a slightly different combination of many of the same elements. But at a molecular level, it's all just particles and intermolecular space.

Together, all this same stuff that's vibrating at different frequencies is made of Quantum Consciousness. When broken down into its quantum level, it's all just energy and shows up experientially in the way it's observed to show up. However, you shouldn't feel all-powerful or be anxious that if you personally stop observing things or people, they will disappear. That cotton sweater in your drawer is not a swirling ball of energy waiting for you to open the drawer to observe it and put it on. If that were so, I'd be observing some gold coins coming out of my drawers and rolling into my pockets! What holds everything together is a level of observation taking place on the position of Quantum Consciousness that is creative, and this is Mind. There is one Mind. It is creative, and each of us individuates Mind into a personal experience.

Dr. James Mellon of the Global Truth Center in Los Angeles defines mind as this: "A kinetic field of pure creative energy that is constantly expanding and creating." He goes on to say, "In quantum terms, we would be the particles, and the space, and everything in between. When consciousness evolves or individuates into an individual, it becomes a specific point of the individuated mind that identifies individually. The individuated mind then uses a tool—the brain—as its connective tissue to communicate. The brain, of course, is connected to the entire body, giving mind even more places to communicate." He finishes by saying, "I believe awareness comes out of the brain and is associated with feelings, health, and brain chemistry. Awareness may seem like consciousness, but it is not. Awareness is the brain's interpretation of consciousness and is highly influenced by the physical."

All this presents a big question: Can I use the observation effect to adjust things in my life that I don't like? Yes, I can. I can also use it to create new scenarios that better fit my desire of what I want my life to be like. If everything in my world is actually one divine entity of Energy from which everything actualizes, what else could that be except Quantum Consciousness or, in theological terms, God? "A house divided cannot stand," and so there must only be one Mind, and our individuated consciousness makes creative use of It. Our personal consciousness must be a single and individuated point of Mind, Universal Consciousness, Quantum Consciousness, God, or any number of other names you can give It. It is beyond space and time and contains all the answers to everything in potentiality. I think different people have been able to use It more powerfully, and I believe we haven't yet begun to understand the creative power that we have over our individual lives through observation.

Language is a means of observation, and it's creative. There is a consciousness in words which is why millions of lives have been transformed by the proper use of daily affirmations.

Feelings are also a form of observation and are extremely creative. Stress is a feeling. How long is the list of diseases you have heard doctors ascribe to stress? Love can also be a feeling. How many people have told stories of being healed by love alone? Feelings are very creative because they are observation.

While I was floating on the tin can in the Mediterranean Sea, I took great measures to not allow myself to feel stressed about my coming move across the country. I firmly believe that if I'd allowed myself to stress out about the move while I was on the ship, as soon as I got home, I'd have been met with an exacting amount of drama equally proportionate to the amount of stress that I'd permitted myself to wallow in. Instead, I emotionally observed the feelings I desired about a new home, and when I felt those feelings in me, I became grateful for the observation. I observed it as if I already owned it and was grateful for it. When I got home, finding a house to buy and making friends in my new hometown could not have been easier. I found a house on the first day and started collecting friends immediately.

I'm learning more and more about how good it is to be naked. It's good to take off the clothing of religiosity and just be the naked image of individuated Quantum Consciousness observing.

Chapter 7

Hypnosis

Have you considered what actually happens to you when you go to a movie theater, and you love the movie? First, before you go, you make the decision to go. Since you've been to the movies before and previously had great success, you go again with the expectation that your movie experience this time will also be successful. Specifically, the experience you seek is to be captured by the movie. You want to be catapulted from your seat in the theater into the lives of the characters. You want to feel an emotional connection and a bond with the people on the screen and their story.

You arrive at the theater, purchase your ticket, and make your way to your seat. You wait somewhat patiently for the pre-movie reels to be finished and for the movie you have chosen to see to begin. The lights finally dim, and it begins. You quickly get to know the characters on the movie screen, possibly identifying with one or more of them, and you even befriend them. The more you become involved with the movie's plot and characters, the more you begin to move into that magical mental state where you have lost all sense of being in a theater. Everything on the screen is engaging your imagination to the point that you are no longer aware of the chair beneath you. You no longer hear the sound of people eating popcorn around you. And when you do hear those normal sounds around you—a baby suddenly crying, a whisper that was too loud—it jerks you into reality so quickly that you feel jarred and irritated. So you refocus your attention and mentally find your way back onto the screen in that other place with your new friends.

While you are watching the movie, something strange happens. You know that everything on the screen is only a story, and those are not real people. You know they are actors. You might even know the actors' real names. And yet, you feel their characters' pain and their joy. You cry with them and laugh with them. Your subconscious mind is accepting the movie as a real event, and your body is fully responding to what's happening on the screen, even though your conscious mind knows you're in a theater watching a movie. It doesn't matter. You've chosen to temporarily put your conscious mind away. You've disengaged your conscious decision-making to such a degree that you allow yourself to physically respond to what you see on the screen. You might grip the chair harder as you see a snake creep out of the empty eye socket of a human skull. You might become more and more rigid, almost twisting out of your seat, as you fixate on that knife's blade slowly coming down the slit between the door and the door frame. You are terrified for your on-screen friend who's holding the doorknob as they desperately try to pull the door shut. But of course, they just can't hold the door quite tightly enough, and that blade is still there. It's slowly coming down toward their hands, and at any moment... they could be killed. You might even know that character is already making a movie sequel, but you still fear their seemingly imminent death anyway.

What is going on with your body during this time? None of this is real. You know it's not real. And yet, you're sweating profusely. Your body is responding as if it's real. Your heart rate is up. Your muscles are tense. This is a hypnotic trance, and it's completely normal.

Modern research tells us that hypnosis is a waking state where you have focused your attention to such a degree that any peripheral awareness is greatly diminished. Along with this hyperfocused state comes a heightened level of suggestibility. This heightened level of suggestibility is why hypnosis is so useful in personal change work.

If you go to the same theater but a different movie—a love story—and you're in the company of someone you're already attracted to, you're likely to experience even more romantic feelings for that person by the end of the film. This is because of the heightened level of suggestibility during a hypnotic trance that happens naturally when you watch a movie. This suggestibility is also the same reason that television ads have always been so successful. Advertisers know the perfect time to suggest you buy their product is while you are sitting all tranced out watching a television show. While sitting there, your unconscious mind is fully alert, and your decision-making, conscious mind is all numbed out. It explains why you might suddenly find yourself looking at a skincare cream when you go to the supermarket. You were in a highly suggestible state when someone suggested you might have aging skin. And you couldn't help but notice that after you put on the face cream, you were smiling. And other people were smiling at you. And you looked like your life was whole and complete. And all this was suggested to you while you were hypnotized by the television!

And then there was that time you got in your car and drove to the supermarket, exactly like you've done a thousand times before. You closed the door of the car and turned the key to start the engine. You put the car in reverse, backed out onto the street, put the car in drive, and pulled away from the house. Then you suddenly realize you're pulling into the parking lot of the supermarket! It was like you teleported, not drove. You don't remember a thing about the seven minutes of driving: the stoplights, the left-hand turn across traffic at a busy boulevard, the interstate, the exit, the stop sign. You entered a very natural state of hypnotic trance the moment you put the car in drive, and you remained in that trance all the way to the store parking lot.

Please notice that in the two examples I've just given of hypnotic trance—driving a car and going to the movie theater—no one is in control of the trance except you. Hypnosis is a natural state and something that we do to ourselves. The movie can lead you into a trance, but it does not control you. You can exit the trance at any moment. The repetition of driving to the store can allow you to slip into a trance. But when that happens, you're doing it to yourself. And if you were ever in a dangerous moment, you'd pop out of it immediately.

When a person goes to a hypnotist, the hypnotist can guide that person into a trance state, but they do not control the person any more than the movie does. The hypnotist always remains a guide and nothing more than a guide. And just like the person driving would immediately pop out of a trance and into complete awareness the second they needed to, the same happens in a hypnosis session. If something did not feel right, the client would simply open their eyes.

Even more important for you is that you can do hypnosis without any kind of guide or hypnotist to guide you. You can do it to yourself through self-hypnosis. And when you know how to do it, the ability to do it regularly is invaluable. When you understand the process of hypnosis, how powerful it is, and how you can do it at a moment's notice, the uses become better and better. You can even do it in a crowded and busy place with your eyes open and without anyone even knowing you are doing it.

Because most people have only seen hypnosis through the eyes of entertainment, they have a complete misperception and misunderstanding of what hypnosis is. The truth of hypnosis in the movies and on television ranks right up there with zombies and vampires. What you see in entertainment about hypnosis is nothing more than made-up stories based on people's fears of being out of control. Yes, it's fun to watch, and no, it doesn't make me mad that they use hypnosis in that way. Sometimes it's fun to be entertained by something as silly as zombies and vampires.

I also love stage hypnosis shows. What fun! Yes, there are people on stage who are hypnotized. A stage show demonstrates the huge range of hypnotic states. Typically in a stage show, the hypnotist will end up with about twenty people on stage. Out of that twenty, there will be four categories of people: the creative, the faker, the zoned out, and the oh-crap-I-wish-I-weren't-up-here people.

During the first part of the show, the hypnotist will send a few people back to their seats. It's not that they can't be hypnotized, it's just that they are too self-aware, and in the moment of being on stage, they fail to relax and focus enough to participate. The oh-crap-I-wish-I-weren't-up-here folks usually start off focusing on the instructions but then get distracted by what they see around them, and they pull out of the trance. But now they are on stage and don't want to be embarrassed by being sent back to their chairs, so they halfway play along. But you can tell they aren't really in a trance.

The zoned-out people are the ones on stage that are really hypnotized, but they let themselves get so caught up in the physical relaxation of being hypnotized that they just don't care about what's going on, and so they're not very entertaining. For some of them, this might be the first time they have ever been that physically relaxed in their entire life. The fact that they're in front of an audience doesn't mean anything to them because they've found a sweet spot to almost nap under a tree, and once there, they do not want to come out and play even if they are on stage. They usually end up looking like they're drugged for most of the show and end up lying across another person or a chair, just zoned out.

The fakers are people who are not hypnotized but, for some personal reason, are totally faking it to show off or because they want to be stars. Yes, you can tell the difference between the fakers and the creatives.

The creatives are the ones who have found that sweet spot. They went into a mentally relaxed state but didn't get so physically relaxed they ended up being zoned-out participants. They found a mentally relaxed trance that allowed them to still be fully energized physically. This trance state has allowed them to become so mentally engaged in focusing on what their hypnosis guide is telling them to experience that they can actually experience it. They know it's not real, just like you know the movies at the theater aren't real. But in that moment, they can still experience it as real. And watching them experience it can be very entertaining.

All four types of participants that volunteered to be on stage did it with the intention and expectation of having fun. The ones that successfully went into that creative trance and remained there were simply more committed to the process and to having fun.

I'll say it again: Trance is natural. While you are reading this right now, if you are focusing on these words, you are currently in a slight reading trance. I've already discussed the movie trance and the driving trance. Now you can easily understand that it happens all the time. You might be like my mother, who has a sewing trance, or my niece, who has a computer-related work trance. My other niece is a nurse in a trauma unit at a very busy hospital. She has her Get-the-hell-out-of-my-way-I'm-handling-an-emergency trance. Here are some other very common trance states: football player trance, tennis trance, dancer trance, test trance, writer trance, cooking trance, vacuuming trance, painting trance, study trance, etc. And since you can now see that trances happen continuously, you can now realize that you can create a trance on purpose for your benefit. You can create a state for yourself now to return to at any time where you are instantly more calm, more relaxed, and more in control.

Anyone can be hypnotized. Every person who sits down with the expectation of learning how to create a trance state of relaxation can do it, especially when they stay committed to learning how to do it. And it's like anything else; the more you practice it, the easier it becomes.

However, it doesn't take much practice to understand it well enough to make some very significant changes in your life.

Well-known author and therapist, Doctor Richard Nongard, teaches this simple exercise in order to give people an experience with a relaxed trance state. It's called Autogenic Training. The prefix auto- means self, and "genic" means to generate. So this is an exercise to give you the experience of generating from within yourself. It won't take much practice to learn this technique. It's extremely powerful in that it easily demonstrates how much control you have over your body. Understanding that you have this kind of control can become really important to people who sometimes feel out of control and express it through eating disorders, smoking, humiliation, or rage.

Read through this exercise so you know what's coming. You can quickly memorize the steps because the order is all parts of the body in close proximity to each other: right arm, left arm, both arms, neck and shoulders, heart, right leg, left leg, both legs, solar plexus, and forehead . . . and finally, just peace. If you are not familiar with the term "solar plexus," it's that space in your gut between your belly button and your rib cage. Do this sitting upright in a chair with your feet on the floor and your hands resting in your lap. Close your eyes while you're doing each step, but if you need to open them to read the next step, that's perfectly fine. You just close them as you do the step and open them again for the next one. Once you have done the exercise a few times and have memorized it, you won't need to open your eyes. The sensations created by this exercise will get stronger and stronger the more you use it.

Autogenic Training

As you say each of these statements three times out loud, with your eyes closed, bring your full awareness into the body parts you are mentioning.

"My right arm is heavy and warm." (Repeat three times out loud.)

"My left arm is heavy and warm." (Repeat three times out loud.)

"Both my arms are heavy and warm." (Repeat three times out loud.)

"My neck and shoulders are heavy." (Repeat three times out loud.)

"My heartbeat is calm and regular." (Repeat three times out loud.)

"My right leg is heavy and warm." (Repeat three times out loud.)

"My left leg is heavy and warm." (Repeat three times out loud.)

"Both my legs are heavy and warm." (Repeat three times out loud.)

"My solar plexus is warm and comfortable." (Repeat three times out loud.)

"My forehead is cool." (Repeat three times out loud.)

"I am at peace." (Repeat three times out loud.)

And I'm sure that after this exercise, you are at peace. Aren't you? That in itself is a powerful feeling to anyone who has ever had to deal with anxiety. It's wonderful to be at peace. Healing is at peace. However, as you will soon learn, there is much more that you can do with this trance state.

Chapter 8

Use Your Brain

To start talking about your ultra amazing brain, here's a list of fun facts:

- The human brain triples in size in the first year.
- Your brain isn't fully developed until age 25.
- The fully developed human brain contains around 100 billion neurons which is about the same number of stars in the Milky Way.
- There are no pain receptors in the brain, so it doesn't feel pain.
- The visual areas of the brain are in the back, not in the front.
- The brain can power a small light bulb with its electrical output, which ranges from 12 to 25 watts.
- Being called a fathead is actually a compliment because, other than water, your brain is mostly fat.

Birth happens. And when it does, everything is fresh and new. We pop out of the womb with a fully functioning brain but not a fully wired brain. We get the privilege of wiring our own brains as we grow to personally fit each of our individual lifestyles. Each individual experience from that first breath onward creates some form of memory and response pattern through the release of brain chemicals and the firing of neural pathways.

We have a continuous loop of information traveling through our bodies via electrical impulses. It's almost like your nervous system acts as a high-speed rail track through your body, and these little high-speed trains send information up and down and all around. These nervous system train tracks are made up of neurons with neurotransmitters all over them. Those neurotransmitters act like junctions and switch back, giving billions of options for the high-speed train. Traveling along the rails of your nervous system, information gets passed from one place to the next, building neural pathways. When a pathway is successful, dopamine is released in your brain, and that feels really good to you. Because of that really good feeling, you will use that pathway again. The more you use that pathway, the stronger that rail system becomes. This dopamine reward system is largely how a toddler learns to get the spoon into their mouth instead of the side of their cheek. When the correct neural pathways are used to achieve proper muscle function, one level of successful dopamine is excreted. As the taste buds develop and more pleasure is experienced, more of the chemical is released. The pleasure chemicals in the brain are extremely powerful. Just watch a baby the first time they taste ice cream! Ice cream causes their taste buds to fire far more than normal and in new ways, which releases loads of chemicals into their brain. And that's why a baby's facial expressions are so cute and exaggerated.

All new motor skills are learned in this exact same way, with the rising and falling of chemicals in the brain. Physical movement creates the possibility of success. When success happens, dopamine is released, and your brain is happy, so you know to use that pathway again. Over and over, the neural pathways are made, and the high-speed train runs. The more our new little brain is active, the quicker these pathways develop. One minute our success was from reaching up and down to victoriously touching our own toes. The next minute success was a first step, then multiple steps. It's easy to witness the power of dopamine when it's triggered not only by personal success but also by parental praise. We struggle with walking at first, but those clapping hands and shouts of joy overload our toddler brain with fantastic chemicals that urge us to repeat those movements until the unconscious mind turns it into a habit. In just a short amount of time and through repetition, it becomes second nature.

Although that amazing and powerful parental praise will continue to have its effect on us for the rest of our lives, eventually, our own desires, emotions, and repeated use will also make use of the high-speed train of information in our body. The neural pathways only grow stronger and stronger. Over time, all these repeated experiences create a self-identifying ego with personality traits and habits. Some of the habits are physical; others become emotional habits. Eventually, it's almost as if your ego has written itself a manual that reads, "When this happens, do and respond like this." And you behave accordingly.

The nervous system is the body's command center and controls all your muscle movement through electrical impulses. Every thought you have impacts your nervous system, which in turn impacts the functioning of your body. This influence from your thoughts goes all the way down to the subconscious mind beating your heart and controlling your breathing, all the way up to a conscious decision to move your arm. Neurophysiologists tell us that when it comes to conscious and even unconscious movement of your body, there is a two-hundredth of a millisecond pause that takes place between the impulse or decision to create movement and the actual movement you create. That's a lot to absorb, so I'll restate it in a different way.

If you take a second and divide it into one thousand equal parts, it would take two hundred of those parts before the decision to move your arm becomes the actual movement. What do I call that two-hundredth of a millisecond pause? I call it "opportunity." There is scientific proof of this split-second opportunity to allow your ego to respond to your brain's manual in a different way, with a different action, with a different behavior. Two-hundredths of a millisecond doesn't sound like much time; however, I'll reframe that time for you into distance.

An electrical impulse in the nervous system travels at speeds of up to three hundred and ninety-four feet per second. That means in a time span of two hundred milliseconds, a nerve impulse can travel almost seventy-nine feet. When turned into physical space, that's a pretty big amount. That's a large enough spot to allow you some creativity for a new decision and a whole lot of opportunity for change through hypnosis and basic naked prayer. You have the room to make new decisions and choices, break old habits, and develop new ones.

I was brimming with rage as a forty-year-old man. It wasn't until my late thirties that I started to psychologically deal with what had happened to me as a child, a young adult, and then as a young man. I had been abused by my father, shamed as a child, lied to as a young adult, and disowned as a young man. All this happened to me in the name of religion because I didn't fit into the Evangelical theology of who could actually be "saved." My sin was considered too grievous. I just dropped all sense of spiritual development and did what I wanted to do.

When I finally managed to make it to middle age, I felt a desire to begin again looking inside myself and continue the development of my spiritual life. In order to do that, I knew I had to start with forgiveness. I had a list of rage triggers a mile long. Some of them were as silly as picking up a hairdryer every morning to use. As soon as I had that hairdryer in my hand, all I could hear was my father telling me how sissified it was to use a blow-dryer. To him, I was a sissy. Just hearing the word *church* would immediately change my mood. It took several years of determination and many days of failure before I found successful methods that worked for me, giving me the tools to create change within that two-hundredth of a millisecond space my brain had given me. I never went to a hypnotist, but out of pure fascination for the subject, I started to study it. It was during my times of study that I constantly had light-bulb moments of realization: "This is what I did." I know from personal experience that two hundred milliseconds or seventy-nine feet is enough space to make new decisions and develop new habits. But I admit it takes a lot of commitment to the process. All good things come from commitment.

Definitions of words are always important. Without strong definitions, conversations about complex subjects can become a dance of semantics. When you're dancing in semantics, it's hard to know which meaning of a word the author is using. Interpreters between languages struggle all the time with semantics. But with the English language, we have many words that are used to mean different things in different contextual circumstances, which can create even more confusion. *Mind*, *brain*, and *consciousness* are three of those words. Those words are like tightly intertwined cords that form one rope. But in truth, they each have different meanings. They should not be used interchangeably because they do not mean the same thing.

We experience the brain as physical matter. It's not a muscle, even though we claim to exercise it like one. It's fatty in makeup and comprised of various organs that produce chemicals that describe our feelings which we interpret into emotions. It creates and controls electric impulses that run our entire body on all three levels of the mind: conscious, unconscious, and subconscious.

The mind is something else entirely. We do not experience the mind as physical, but instead as a process. We mainly experience the mind as individuated, which is an individual, personal use of the one Mind. We also experience an individuated consciousness, which is individuated from the singular Quantum Consciousness. In his book, *The Everything Answer Book*, Amit Goswami says, "Thus consciousness is not a phenomenon of the brain. In the quantum view, consciousness is the ground of all being, and the brain is a phenomenon of consciousness." I will restate Mr. Goswami adding personal words in parenthesis, different punctuation, and some capitalization to provide an easier interpretation of what I believe he is saying. "Thus consciousness (individuated) is not a phenomenon of the brain. In the quantum view, Consciousness (God) is the ground of all being. And the brain is a phenomenon of (individuated) consciousness."

Your mind is an individuated use of the one Mind, a higher level of an energy of intelligence that your brain connects to and uses in an individuated experience. Your brain is a tool that's used by the mind for physical experience and expression. Your mind is using your brain to pump information through your body and into your experience in a similar way that your heart pumps blood through your body. Information, inspiration, and intuition are all pumped through your individuated use of Mind into your personal mind and then brought into awareness by your tool of a brain to create conscious use, unconscious use, and subconscious use.

I have repeatedly heard New Age metaphysicians say, "Change your thinking, change your life." There is a tremendous amount of truth in that saying. The problem I've always struggled with in that saying is the experiential question that naturally follows it, "How?" How do you change your thinking? In the community of hypnosis and neuro-linguistic programming, you will hear a similar phrase that answers the question, "How?" The phrase is, "Change your words, change your brain, change your life."

Neuropsychologist Rick Hanson teaches in his book, *Buddha's Brain*, "When your mind changes, your brain changes too . . . What flows through your mind sculpts your brain." We know this is true because we know on a scientific level how the development of the brain is achieved in toddlers through those billions of high-speed, train-like neural pathways. We know these pathways are created by what you think, feel, say, and do. Many of them are so deep and so natural that they slip into the unconscious mind becoming habitual patterns of feeling, speaking, and doing. In order to change your thinking, you have to choose new words. This simple but sometimes challenging act will help you to think differently. New words will change how you feel and how you respond. As you can now see, just by changing your words, you have completely broken the previous neural pathway. New words create new pathways and literally change the brain. When your new word is used over and over, it will eventually slip into the unconscious mind replacing the old habit with a new one.

Another great teacher of brain science was psychologist Donald Hebb. He first wrote in 1949, "Neurons that fire together wire together." He taught us that we can create new mental pathways and strengthen them through repetition.

In Chapter 6, I talked about Quantum Consciousness and the power of observation. Many forms of observation are very powerful: visualization, meditation, memory, study, feelings, emotion, imagination, and words. All these forms of observation change the brain. When you change your brain, you change your use of your own mind, which changes the brain even more. This dynamic and ongoing loop of observation and change is very creative. This is wonderful news and can be a powerful catalyst for producing the changes we want in our lives. But also remember that creativity can be viewed from our life perspective as destruction. For instance, cancer destroys our lives, but cancer is a creation. Even though it destroys our bodies and our lives, it has emerged out of a process of creativity.

Our well-defined laserlike point of view is what makes our words and our language patterns such a powerful form of observation. When you change your words and language patterns, it changes your point of view and gives you a new point of observation. Observing is creating. When you look for new things, new things appear. When you say things differently, different outcomes are created. This is a powerful realization and a tremendously useful concept that gives you much more personal control over your life. Words are hypnotic in nature, and they are all a natural form of prayer that requires no religious clothing. They represent your naked consciousness reaching into Quantum Consciousness and creating newness from an observation. You need no religion to do this; you were created this way.

Feelings and emotions are also very creative means of creating. These two words are often used interchangeably, and yet there are subtle differences between feelings and emotions. Feelings are something you experience internally. They can be mental states. For example, you can feel sadness, happiness, anger, fear, or love. The psychological and physiological expressions of your feelings, whether conscious or unconscious, can be emoted; therefore, they become emotions. Facial expressions and physiological changes like heart rate or breathing rate are all manifestations of an emotion that your body is emoting. I'm sure you can easily guess which one is more creative—feelings or emotions. When your body is impacted by feelings to such a degree that it emotes, it becomes an observation that is very powerful. Stress creates a full array of change in the body. Most disease has a direct creative relationship with stress. Gratefully, we also have joy which is also very creative and healing in nature. The observational power of emotions tends to be very connected to some form of trigger: a person, an experience, a memory, a word, a place, etc. These triggers are connected to neural pathways in the brain that produce chemicals. Repeated use of these triggers creates emotional habits. How wonderful to know that there is a two-hundredth of a millisecond—nearly seventy-nine feet—in which we get to choose to emote or not to emote.

Your imagination is also extremely creative. Everything that we see in our modern world started as an imagined thing. Even when we remember a specific experience that actually happened to us, in the process of remembering, it becomes imagined because it's not happening in the now. It has to be reimagined to be remembered. Because of this, your imagination is also a very powerful tool that you can use to prepare yourself for future experiences. You can use your imagination to practice how you will respond in circumstances you know are certain to be in your future. Before they even happen, you can practice over and over until you have already created a strong neural pathway for the reaction you choose to act out.

One of the ways athletes become better and better at performing their sport is by imagining themselves playing the game and winning. Professional basketball players visualize shooting a basketball into the hoop from every possible place they could be on the court, even when they're not on that court. Football players visualize their plays. Quarterbacks practice feeling themselves throw. Golfers mentally practice their game and how they want to feel when they strike the ball. I play the piano, and many times friends have caught me with my fingers moving on a table or my lap and someone would ask me, "What musical piece are you playing in your head right now?"

I'll give you another quote from Rick Hanson in *Buddha's Brain:* "When an intention crystalizes, your inner experience of things coming together toward a unified aim reflects a neural coherence." He goes on to say that regions of the brain "start pulsing together, matching the phases—the highs and lows—of their firing rhythms." When I read his description of intention crystalizing and the brain pulsing together, I was immediately reminded of a teaching by famed theologian Ralph Waldo Emerson. He said, "Once you make a decision, the Universe conspires to make it happen."

Imagining and reimagining are tremendously powerful tools that give you the ability to effectively pray completely naked of any religious cloth, special religious words, or special beliefs about "God's will." Hypnosis makes grand use of these very creative observational powers to create skill and opportunity. Self-hypnosis places that power into your own hands to be used continuously. You have the power. You can use it.

Chapter 9

Hypnosis vs. Prayer

I can sit down, place my hands on my legs, raise the pointer finger of my right hand and then let it fall back down onto my leg and immediately go into a light state of trancelike bliss. I can do it with my eyes closed or my eyes open. My shoulders will drop down away from my ears, and automatically my heart rate will begin slowing down. My forehead will relax, and my ears will lower. In that light trance, I can put a smile on my face and immediately change the chemistry of my brain. I know how to do this, and I do it regularly. I do it in the doctor's office. I do it while sitting in traffic. I did it on that Sunday while I was sitting in church, hearing the minister screaming about the evil homosexuals who are ruining his country. This is self-hypnosis, and it's wonderful. It can also be interpreted as a form of prayer if used well.

The origins of hypnosis are mostly connected to a German physician named Franz Anton Mesmer. He developed the idea of *mesmerism* which is where we get the word "mesmerized." But people fail to mention that Mesmer was a student of a Catholic priest named Maximilian Hell. That is not a joke, and what a hell of a name for a priest! Throughout the next two centuries, the work of Hell and Mesmer was carried on by multiple doctors and went through multiple versions of praise and vilification. As the quest for chemical healing gained momentum in the medical field, many dismissed hypnosis as only a placebo effect. But regardless of the dismissal, people continued to be healed. During this period of history, we discovered there is tremendous power in the mind, not only for knowledge but also for healing. Today we continue this quest with modern medicine to explore the power of our own minds. I'm especially curious as to what exactly that power is, from where it comes, and how we harness it. Isn't that the purpose of not only hypnosis but also of prayer?

Like Father Hell, church leaders have always worked to develop successful techniques to grow and control their churches. When they discover what works, they use it and repeat it. Pastors do not begin their Sunday mornings with the direct intention of hypnotizing their congregations. But due to its own developed nature, the church is an inescapably hypnotic place and experience. A church can produce feelings and experiences that are real, powerful, and also placebo-like. It's fascinating to see how traditional church services mirror the components of a visit to a clinical hypnotist session.

It's important for you to understand there are four important criteria necessary for hypnosis to have a strong effect. Those criteria are the beliefs, convictions, and expectations of the client. The fourth is the medium by which those three things are best expressed—imagination. And interestingly, those first three criteria—belief, conviction, and expectation—are the primary reasons people go to church.

Imagination

Imagination is a form of observation, and so it's very creative. In hypnosis, we engage the client's imagination to change the unconscious habit patterns created by the neural pathways in the brain. Imagination is important in hypnosis because it provides the medium for a new belief and a new outcome. Your imagination should also be fully engaged when you pray. How can you pray with true conviction that you have the outcome of your prayer if you cannot imagine what it would be like to live inside that outcome?

Regardless of the motivation—fear or love, desperation or gratitude, certainty or uncertainty—it's impossible to ponder the topic of God without fully engaging the power of your imagination. It's set in motion the moment you see the church doors. They use your imagination to teach you what is considered a proper response to the world around you. They teach you how you should feel and respond to people, places, and things. And yet, they rarely engage your imagination with a positive outcome for your prayers. Sermons are full of imaginings about life after death— heaven or hell, nothingness, or an eternity of elation versus eternal pain. All these imaginings directly influence both your unconscious and subconscious thinking and action. But rarely would someone pray sitting in an active imagination about the success of their prayers. The best you are given is hope. "If it's God's will."

Symbols are the language of imagination, and you're pounded with them the moment you step into a church. Artwork, stained glass, and statues are all begging for your attention in stories of both hope and despair. The speakers' podium, the kneeling benches, the hymnals in the pews, and the baptistry are all calling for your obedience while the sounds of the organ and the smells of the incense try to massage you into compliance. If you take communion, the textures and tastes all have symbolic meaning that speaks directly to your unconscious and automated habits of right and wrong. Your imagination is on fire and seeking ways to express the other three hypnotic components: belief, conviction, and expectation. How would prayer be different if you stopped begging and started imagining positive outcomes? What would happen to your prayer if you created within yourself the feelings of success and just remained in that feeling?

Belief

Beliefs are the tenets we live by, the cognitive mental acceptance that something is real or true. It's a mental construct through which we observe our past and present to predict our future. It's clear that our beliefs are a form of observation that are very creative.

Eventually, beliefs make it past the cognitive conscious mind and down into the unconscious, where they become the unspoken automated control knobs that govern our actions. They also either clog or clear our conscience regarding our actions. If someone believes in the power of prayer, then miracles are possible. If someone believes in hypnosis, then self-change is possible.

A good hypnotist knows that in order to create change in a person's life, their client must change their beliefs about the issue they're presenting, whether it be an emotional or physical habit. When they believe things can be different, the road goes from dirt to gravel. The more that new outcome is practiced with success, the more the road eventually becomes paved into automation.

We gather our beliefs from so many different places that are unique to our life experiences. The majority of our population draws a large portion of their beliefs from either a direct relationship to church teaching or a handed-down version. The secondhand version comes from parents, grandparents, teachers, etc.—important and influential authorities in our lives who have a direct relationship with the church. This makes the influence of the church impossible to escape in our culture. In general, most people who attend church also believe that their priest or pastor is in some way a representative of God. It's a common tradition among Evangelical Christians to say that their pastor is actually speaking "the word of God." That phrase alone has hypnotic and deep psychological implications because it superimposes the prestige of the ultimate authoritarian power.

For some people, prestige is a powerfully hypnotic influencer. It's used in sales tactics all the time. Prestige is the hallmark of luxury brands on items like cars, clothing, jewelry, and even timeshare vacations. You'll remember my personal story from earlier in this book when Mrs. Brown said to me, "If it's in the book." It's possible that Mrs. Brown didn't feel enough prestige within herself to tell me I was a sinner, so she gave deference to a much more prestigious authority, "the book."

When someone makes the claim of "Speaking the word of God," they are giving a direct hypnotic suggestion that God is speaking directly to you, the listener; there is no more ultimate prestige than that. It's a level of prestige so strong that it can decimate the critical thinking skills in the conscious mind of a believer, forcing them to accept this word of God on unsubstantiated faith alone. And when that happens, it goes directly into your unconscious thinking and continuously expresses itself through unconscious automated acts and habits.

In very old styles of hypnosis, a hypnotist will rely on the client's belief, usually drawn from entertainment venues, that the hypnotist alone is in control of what they think and do while under hypnosis. By using this strategy, it creates a position of authority for the hypnotist—a level of prestige that can cause change. It actually works very well with certain personality types, but it's not for everyone, and I personally don't think of it as healthy. That style of hypnosis also raises the question, "But what of self-hypnosis?" If the power of prestige is necessary to change, how do you use self-hypnosis? How do you become your own prestige authority? It might answer the question as to why people who pray in a begging manner rarely sit and imagine their success. They are not their own prestige authority but are always in search of a savior.

Conviction

Conviction plays a strong role in hypnosis. How strongly do you want to quit smoking, lose weight, stop biting your nails, or give that great public speech? Conviction is the critical ingredient that can turn "trying and hoping" into "doing." Conviction is, in some ways, like glue: it holds things together. In this way, conviction is a powerful means of observation that is creative. In fact, it's one of the key components of any success story. The strength and drive to achieve are powered by a belief in what is possible. Without strong convictions, climbing Mount Everest, flying an airplane, or even running a four-minute mile would have forever remained impossible. Strong convictions about what is possible have changed history forever and changed the face of the globe. However, there's nothing quite as strong as religious conviction.

Religious conviction can overcome and defy all logic and common sense. And interestingly, for some people, the stronger their religious conviction, the more complete their church experience will be. Someone who has a strong sense of religious conviction will be convinced that the entire church service was "filled with the Holy Spirit" and sanctioned by the absolute "truth of God." That level of religious conviction becomes the motivating factor for taking time away from their family and attending the services week after week.

The true religious devotee is completely convinced that the eyes of their God are constantly upon them and their every action. He is continuously taking notes about their feelings and actions, and He will use those notes in the final judgment of their life. That judgment will determine their destination for all eternity: heaven or hell, bliss or agony, a position in the heavenly choir, or playing drums in the devil's jazz combo.

However, when used properly, a good sense of healthy conviction will enhance personal motivation and greatly increase focus. A strong, healthy conviction will provide more and more energy toward the achievement of a person's goals. In the hypnosis community, there's a tremendous conviction that hypnosis works, and we see great successes because of that conviction.

Expectation

What are you watching for? What are you looking for? Are you watching for good or looking for defeat? Are you watching for healthy change or for the other shoe to drop? In the process of hypnosis, you can create a greater sense of expectation by choosing what you want to experience instead of looking for more of what you're currently experiencing. Through quieting the mind and engaging your imagination, you can practice the feelings you've chosen to such a degree that an expectation of those feelings happening naturally is created. The realization then begins to unfold into lived reality because you're looking for it to happen. You're observing your world, creating your world, and you expect to see it.

We develop expectations for ourselves from an entire plethora of life experiences. The cultural norms of the society in which we were born automatically define many of our expectations. The level of our family's wealth and position in that community, our personal success and failures as young people, and even the media choices that we continue to listen to give us belief, conviction, and expectation about the potentiality of our lives. We are continuously forced to quietly ask ourselves, "What can I really expect from me?" Expectation is hypnotic because what you look for shows up. If you're looking for the worst, something of that nature will always be in front of you. If you're continuously looking for good, you will always find something good even in the most horrible circumstances. In recognizing our expectations in this way, it should be obvious how powerful it is as a force of creative observation, as well as a great predictor of the future.

Religious convictions also lead to strong expectations. One very strong expectation is to feel something. People want to "feel the spirit." Many people will go to church for that one expectation alone—they expect to feel the spirit. Religious convictions and beliefs also create expectations for the judgment of God. Many pray for the judgment of God to come down upon the evildoers of the world.

Meanwhile, the devoted also expect personal forgiveness from God and some level of protection for themselves.

One of the biggest differences between hypnosis and prayer has to do with self-worth. In hypnosis, the practitioner is going within the deepest caves of their self and creating the change they want to see within their self. There is no begging or asking. Instead, there is decision, motivation, and a sense of power that you're naturally connected to—that is within you. Self-worth is powerful if you pray in a begging manner. Do you really have enough self-worth to come before a punishing God on bended knee and beg for change? Do you believe God is willing to help you change, or is the change you seek not "His will?" Prayer can be a wonderful and powerful experience for some. It can be a glorious and enlightening experience. Others find it daunting, a practice full of shame and guilt, and nearly impossible.

When you decide to pray naked with hypnosis and through simple forms of observation, all the begging and pleading, promises of good behavior in the future, shame, and inability to live up to church standards go away. Praying naked gives you the opportunity to do what is natural to human expression—to an individuated mind and consciousness. It provides you the opportunity to guiltlessly close your eyes, calm your mind, choose something new, and observe it in reality.

Chapter 10

Hypnotic Techniques in Church

Focused attention becomes an opportunity for trance. Whenever you become singularly focused, nature takes over, and trance happens. Most movie or television directors and writers have never studied hypnosis or hypnotic techniques. They don't need to because, by nature, the elements of hypnosis are already present in good storytelling.

The same is true of a well-designed church service. Most church leaders are completely ignorant of hypnosis and the power of its techniques. Not only do they not have the intention, but they also don't possess the knowledge to purposefully implement hypnotic techniques in their church services, but they are powerfully present. It's simply that the techniques used in church services—the practices that have proven themselves to work—are by nature hypnotic. A meaningful service will have the ups and downs, the highs and lows, and the pacing of a well-told story. Since religious trance creates religious conviction and because it's a phenomenon that's so strong and powerful that it's influenced the trajectories of entire nations, it has been studied by anthropologists, psychologists, cultists, religion experts, and even medical doctors for centuries.

To understand this power, I want to compare the steps of a traditional hypnosis session with those of a traditional church service. In putting these two experiences side by side, you will see how similar they are, and it will become more apparent how hypnosis plays a role in the church service.

When you go to a hypnotist, they will typically take you through a set of experiential stages similar to this format:

1. Introduction or pre-talk
2. Induction
3. Deepening
4. Suggestion
5. Emerge

I'll go through each of these stages of a hypnosis session and show a church service equivalent. I'll purposefully use the words *belief, conviction,* and *expectation* in these comparisons to point out when the criteria for hypnotic change that I discussed in Chapter 9 are present.

Stage 1: Introduction or Pre-Talk for Hypnosis

The first encounter with the hypnotist is an opportunity to build rapport, trust, and a commonality that allows their relationship to develop. During this first meeting, many of the questions a client has about hypnosis will be answered, and the hypnotist will begin to have a deeper understanding of the client's needs. Any fears that the client has about hypnosis can be addressed and put aside at this time. It's a perfect opportunity for the hypnotist and client to settle in together and create the first bonds of a trusting relationship.

While building this trust, the hypnotist has the opportunity to discover not just the needs of the client but also the underlying beliefs the client has about their life and the issue they want to change. It's also the best opportunity for the hypnotist to build a new level of conviction about the possibilities that are available to the client and to develop new expectations about their future.

Stage 1: Introduction or Pre-Talk for Church

Here, the introduction creates rapport on many levels. Not only between the churchgoer and the leadership of the church but also the other attendees and even the building itself. Most people don't go to church just for the sermon; they also want to hear inspiring music, they desire a like-minded community, and they even seek an indescribable sensory perception of the building when they first walk in. This is especially true for the first-time attendee. They bring an entire mental list of expectations, and whether conscious or unconscious, they mentally check those expectation boxes one by one. The more boxes that get checked, the more rapport is built with the church they consider attending regularly.

Some of those rapport-building boxes built into the experience include:

Is music being played?

What kind of music is it and do I like it?

Is there someone to greet me and make me feel welcome?

Did I like them?

Do I see a place where I think I will feel comfortable sitting?

Is the temperature okay?

Do I hear people talking pleasantly?

Is it contemplative, or is it active?

Are there smiling faces around me?

Do people here seem happy?

Do I have information in my hand to tell me what's about to happen?

Does the priest/pastor/minister look happy?

Do other people in the building appear satisfied with life?

The answers to all these questions and a host of others answer the question of rapport as well as expectation.

For the regular attendee, this repeated introduction experience becomes very personal as they start developing relationships with other members of the church and look forward to seeing them weekly. They may feel a bond with the church leader and look forward to seeing them. All these feelings create a positive rapport with expectation. The longer the rapport exists and is grown and nurtured, the deeper the rapport grows. Eventually, a strong enough rapport will transform into a deep trust, and the introduction stage melts right into an induction. When that happens, the regular attendee will begin entering their trance experience as early as arriving at the church or even possibly at home while dressing for the service.

Stage 2: The Induction for Hypnosis

Hypnotic induction is a process that hypnotists use to guide their clients into a trance state. There are several types and levels of hypnotic trance, just as there are many forms of natural trance discussed earlier in this book. Hypnotists may use a closed-eye trance, which is especially good for engaging the client's imagination. Or they may use an open-eyed trance, usually called a waking trance, to simultaneously engage the client's conscious and unconscious minds about their beliefs around the topic the client is addressing. And sometimes, both will be used at different points in the session for different purposes. Regardless of the trance type, there's a process or induction that the hypnotist will employ to get the client into their trance.

Some common types of induction are: eye fixation, progressive relaxation, guided imagery, rapid induction, hand-levitation, confusion, breathing, and of course, self-hypnotic induction.

Because repetition breeds expectation, people who see a hypnotist over a long period of time may start to go into trance just walking into the hypnotist's office or, in today's world, when they start their Zoom session. They have rapport and trust with the hypnotist and know what's expected of them—to go into trance. On a subtle level, the client has developed an automated response by simply putting themselves into a trance. This automatic trance response increases with effectiveness through repetition, and they may begin to enter trance even before the session starts.

Stage 2: The Induction for Church

Regular church attendees also have the same automated response, which is ingrained in their unconscious minds. Every time they attend their church, the familiar building, symbolic artwork, sounds, smells, and the friends around them develop a routine that leads to habitual patterns of hypnotic behavior that even determine where they will sit, which is usually in the same place every week. This self-induced mental conditioning is caused by repetitive behavior, which leads to faster trance induction and quicker access to the unconscious and subconscious minds.

Eye fixation can cause a person to slip into a trance. In a movie, people's eyes are fixed on the screen. While driving, people's eyes are fixed on the road in front of them. And when people are sitting around a campfire, their eyes become fixed on the flames. In many churches, you'll find a religious symbol that's presented as a focal point. It'll be lifted high at the front of the room—a statue or piece of artwork. Staring up at this art and fixating your eyes on it can cause a naturally occurring hypnotic trance.

Music is an extremely effective tool for inducing a trance state. There's a strong chance you've seen the power of music at events and concerts. People sway and raise their hands to the music. They even sing along and seem to lose themselves in the moment. The nature of music is to inspire, relax, convince, guide, and even manipulate our thoughts and emotions. The magic of music is that it engages us on all levels of the mind: conscious, unconscious, and subconscious.

Prelude music in a church before a service always aids in progressive relaxation. It sets an atmosphere of expectation and gently massages the listeners' subconscious into a relaxation that thins the critical thinking facilities. With the thinning of critical thinking, logic is suspended, which allows messages to flow directly into the unconscious mind.

Congregational singing creates a sense of unity with the whole. While the nature of music is to break down the critical thinking of the conscious mind, hymns and unified singing are the perfect opportunity to teach the beliefs of the church, with everyone singing in agreement. This unified teaching technique creates a tremendous sense of conviction and expectation around specific dogmatic beliefs. These are powerful yes-sets where everyone is expressing agreement. This technique becomes especially powerful at driving unconscious automated emotional responses deep into the human psyche if it's a song that's repeated weekly, such as a church theme.

Another way to officially induce the trance is through an opening prayer or invocation. A client going to a hypnotist expects at some point to hear the hypnotist say, "Now, close your eyes and just listen to my voice." This is exactly what happens with an invocation at a church. The congregation is asked to close their eyes and listen to the prayer. By this time in the service, the imaginations of its congregants are fully engaged while their minds are in a relaxed state of altered consciousness. When the prayer is over, the induction is complete, and trance has been established.

If you are bold enough to look around the congregation after an invocation, you'll notice congregants will have slumped shoulders and see visible signs of relaxation. You'll see flushing on some of their faces, a smoothing of facial muscles, and some with very slacked, relaxed jaws.

You can witness people gazing with unfocused eyes and many with slightly dilated pupils. You'll notice slowed breathing and hear occasional sighs. All these are the physical signs of a light hypnotic trance.

Stage 3: Deepeners for Hypnosis

Our brains send out fluctuating brainwave patterns that are measurable. For instance:

13–30 Hz. Beta Waves. Waking state.

8–12 Hz.   Alpha Waves. Light trance.

3–7 Hz.   Theta Waves. Deeper trance.

0.5–3 Hz.   Delta Waves. Sleep.

Giving out beta waves means we're fully in a waking state. Delta waves mean we're fully asleep. But during alpha and theta, our critical thinking has been slightly diminished, and as a general rule, we're most open to suggestibility and physical responses to our own imagination.

Depending on the style of the hypnotist, the personality of the client, and even the reason the client is seeing the hypnotist, a hypnotist will use an induction to guide the client into a light state of trance. A deepener can be used to go into a deeper state if it's advantageous. Sometimes it is, and sometimes it isn't. This is where the skill of the hypnotist is very valuable. But just because a person has their eyes open doesn't mean they're in a beta state. They might actually be much deeper.

Taking a client deeper into a state of trance can facilitate them in becoming more open to suggestion and to the changes they want to make in their life. In this deepened state, the critical thinking of the brain hasn't been shut off, but it has been dimmed. These deeper states are wonderful for changing beliefs, creating stronger convictions, and growing greater expectation. In these deeper states, habits can be changed, and even new ones developed. It's in these deeper states that an athlete can develop greater skills because they're actually addressing what they believe is possible for themselves. They can create more conviction within themselves about their abilities, and because of that stronger conviction, they have a greater expectation that's brought to life and fulfilled in their various sports.

I mentioned yes-sets earlier when talking about the power of unified singing. Repeated compliance and yes-sets are not only good rapport builders for salespeople, but if rapport is already established, they function as great techniques to deepen a hypnotic trance. When you encounter a well-trained salesperson, they'll quickly attempt to establish likability and commonality (rapport) with you. They'll begin this process with a couple of very simple compliance steps:

"Please sit here."

And you comply.

"Here is some water for you."

You comply by just taking the water. Even more so if you take a sip.

And then they establish the yes-sets. This is a simple communication principle that's taught in all sales trainings. It has been established by psychology that once someone agrees with you at least three times, they're more likely to continue accepting what you say as true and agreeing with you. It doesn't matter what they're agreeing with you about; it may be a totally different subject. Just the act of agreeing is enough.

I used to sell timeshares. Once you were in my office and I told you where to sit and offered you water, I might begin with:

"Great weather for June, isn't it?"

"Yes."

"Is that your blue car I saw in the parking lot?"

"Yes, it is."

"I saw it was a Honda. They make such a reliable product, don't they?"

"Yes, they do."

You've agreed with me three times. There's now a greater likelihood that you'll continue to agree with me. Public speakers use this technique. Any good therapist, and especially a good hypnotist, will also use these techniques. They're often used in the introduction stage to help create rapport, but if rapport is already established, they'll act as a deepener to solidify the rapport and the trance.

Compliance in a therapist's or doctor's office:

"Please take a seat there in the chair opposite me."

"I need you to please sign this piece of paper just saying you are here today."

Yes-set:

"Wow, did you notice how nice the weather is today?"

"Yes."

"And I see you arrived a little early today!"

"Yes."

"Are you ready to begin?"

"Yes."

Stage 3: Deepeners for Church

You can also find a lot of compliance builders and yes-sets in a church service and in the sermon. Compliance is achieved by the social pressure of having people stand and sit to sing certain hymns. Kneeling for certain prayers, making the sign of the cross at specific times, and participating in a congregational call and response are all natural compliance builders, and this compliance will naturally deepen the trance state of the congregants.

Quite possibly the greatest compliance builder I have seen in church, which also acts as a tremendous deepener, is the taking of communion. With a given signal, all the believers stand and get in a single file line to pass by the priest, receive communion, and then walk back to their seats. It's done obediently and without question, with faces that are emotionless and dazed, fully displaying hypnotic trance identifiers. When they come before the priest, he places a wafer on their tongue. Somewhere between the wafer leaving their tongue and entering their stomach, it's believed to change into the actual flesh of Jesus. This transformation is called transubstantiation.

While in Spain, I spoke with a brother and sister about their experience of communion. They both loved the act of communion. The sister found great importance in the symbology of communion. She felt it was a symbolic demonstration of unifying the church body, but she didn't believe in transubstantiation—that the wafer literally became the flesh of Jesus. The brother, however, did believe in the full miracle of transubstantiation. He was fully convinced that the wafer became the flesh of Jesus. His proof was that he has a very serious case of celiac disease, and the wafers the church uses are not gluten-free. He accepts the miracle of transubstantiation because he has never had a gluten reaction to communion. How could he when the flesh of Jesus is gluten-free? As much as this plays into my sense of humor, when he told me this, he wasn't joking, and his sister was as wide-eyed as I was!

In the Catholic tradition and in some traditional Black churches, organ music is used throughout the service. The sounds of the organ seem to completely surround and even permeate your body. The use of major and minor keys is a subtle but strong and persuasive communication technique that deepens trance.

Praise songs are now very popular in many modern Protestant churches. Praise songs are rhythmic and extremely repetitive. The simplicity of the melody and the repetitiveness of the lyrics make it easy to get lost in the trancelike feeling of the song. Some people even get dizzy and light-headed. Some experience arm catalepsy, where their arms just seem to effortlessly float in the air. In this environment, you'll also see a lot of swaying bodies and nodding heads. These are all physiological signs of a deep hypnotic trance.

In hypnosis, there's a technique called "fractionation." This method is performed by taking a client into a hypnotic trance, bringing them to a waking state, and then taking them back into trance again. When the client goes back into trance, they'll naturally go even deeper. When you're at the movie theater and something jars you out of the story, notice that when you turn your attention back to the screen and return to the story, you go even deeper into the scene with a greater focus. Sports coaches have used this technique as a pattern interrupt when their players have lost momentum and started a streak of bad plays. How many games have you seen where there's a complete turnaround of player energy and focus after halftime? Their halftime off-field pep talk can be very persuasive.

Possibly the most effective deepener in church is prayer. The more you can get a person to drop their head and close their eyes, silence their own thinking, and allow someone else to speak for them, the deeper into a trance they will go.

Stage 4: Suggestion for Hypnosis

You have been receiving suggestions since you were born. Some of the messages were direct, and some were indirect. Some of them were good, and some were devastating. Together, the good and bad have molded the trajectory of your entire life. These messages came from your parents, grandparents, teachers, pastors, siblings, friends, and your culture. They were received by your conscious mind, and through repetition, many of those messages slowly seeped into your unconscious beliefs about who you are. They have been in full active mode, working in the background of your daily life, regulating your automated unconscious reactions to everything you encounter.

You were told you were smart, dumb, good, bad, talented, pretty, handsome, ugly, evil, angelic, funny, valued, a blessing, and/or a bother. Through these messages from multiple sources, your young brain and, gradually, your unconscious mind started forming your self-image and self-worth. Hypnotically, in a defining trajectory, you began believing the specific details others described you because you also began to observe these descriptions in yourself. And the more of it you saw, the more of it there was to see, and the more of it you created.

During a hypnosis session, the suggestion stage is full of multiple techniques that apply both direct and indirect messaging because everyone responds differently to specific styles of learning. You might hear direct suggestions being stated from an authoritative position and providing a new truth for the client to believe as an absolute fact about themselves. "You are now a nonsmoker" would be considered a direct suggestion. This can be a very powerful method of change when the suggestions are positive and repeated in multiple ways throughout the session. But they are most powerful if the client has a trusting relationship and a good rapport with the hypnotist.

Indirect suggestions are also very powerful, and some agree even more powerful ways to manipulate the unconscious mind. We hear indirect suggestions about ourselves our entire lives. We learn to interpret and respond to indirect suggestions very early in life. Even toddlers notice how people look at them when they enter a room. And as our minds develop, we start to draw indirect suggestions about who we are from multiple sources: metaphors, stories, presuppositions, ambiguity, imagery, and symbols. All these set our imaginations on fire for creative neural pathway construction. So naturally, indirect suggestion is a brilliant technique to use during hypnosis sessions to create newness in our self-image and personal value.

Stage 4: Suggestion for Church

Many churches have special music, which is usually meant to evoke a strong emotional response. One hypnotist I spoke with said, "Making a person emotional is like digging the garden and getting it ready to plant the seeds." Well-performed special music is an excellent trance deepener to use right before the sermon, and it will be full of suggestions—both direct and indirect.

After the rapport building of the prelude music, the comfort of their regular place to sit, the greeting from like-minded people, an induction of praise songs, the unification of hymn singing, the deepening of trance through special music, and the fractionation that takes place during all this with opening and closing the eyes during prayers, the congregants should be in a fully induced waking trance. Now that everyone is in this trance state, a preacher uses direct suggestion to plant the seeds of their message about humanity directly into the unconscious and subconscious minds of their listeners. Repetition in decades of sermons is deeply effective at planting, watering, and reaping these strongly established beliefs. And, of course, all this is made even more effective by using it as a prestige tool called "the word of God."

Listen for yes-sets in a sermon. Once the Amens begin rolling in, they won't stop.

"God is good."

"Amen."

"God loves you."

"Amen."

"God wants to give you all the desires of your heart."

"Amen."

"But at your core, you are an evil sinner who needs to be saved."

"Amen."

Stories of despair are a great way to illustrate the woes of going against the teachings and dogma of the church. Then hearing about others' successes as a follow-up can be a dynamic tool to create tremendous conviction around a set of beliefs and to set expectations in the ears of the listener.

All forms of religion have a call to action that acts as the ultimate compliance set. Compliance might be found in weekly confession or an altar call to "receive Christ." Compliance becomes an act of submission to the teaching. It's giving up personal power to another authority outside yourself. It's always based in a fear of what might happen and is delivered when the listener is in a state of trance, emotional, and has their critical thinking in a lowered state. Belief, imagination, expectation, and conviction are playing out at their strongest levels in these moments of church "worship."

Stage 5: Emerge for Hypnosis

Emerging is a significant moment in hypnosis because it's the time when you acknowledge the change you were seeking has been made. A new observation has been completed, and you are emerging fresh and changed. The client is guided out of the trance state, taking care to leave the change intact. And even though the hypnosis session is technically over, emerging is an important moment. It's the moment to solidify that what you experienced in your trance state is now your new self, your new identity, and your new trajectory forward.

Depending on the depth of trance, during emergence, you might feel a little groggy, almost as if waking up from a daydream or a nap. During this time, the client is still highly suggestible, and it's important for this to be a positive moment before sending them on their way.

Stage 5: Emerge for Church

At church, some type of official ending to the service is given so that the congregation knows it's time to emerge from their trance. It may be a prayer or a song. Sometimes it will be another unified call and response. Many churches take their offering at this time while the congregation is still in a very suggestible state. It's also the preferred time to make announcements for future events and classes because the congregants are more open to making a decision about returning during this time.

I love a great closing ceremony in a Catholic or Episcopal church that has a grand pipe organ. The organist knows it's time to wake people up and send them out with an energetic blast of sound. And while in this highly suggestible state, this lively music is a subtle message to the listener that their problems are much better now. It's a great idea to have someone with a loving presence, possibly the pastor, shake people's hands as they walk out the door, suggesting they are loved, valued, and should return next week.

I will restate again: Few, if any, church worship leaders are trained in hypnosis and use hypnotic techniques to design worship services. But it should be clear, having read this chapter, that simply due to the hypnotic nature of all the elements of a worship service, trance is induced, and hypnosis is taking place.

Chapter 11

How Do I Learn to Pray Naked?

I hit him hard, right in the face, more than once. My hand was red with his blood. The police were called, and friends of mine rushed me away through the crowd before they could get to where we were. I was put in hiding for the rest of that gay pride parade. I don't even remember what the anti-gay, religious slur was that had been written on that sign. I really don't even have a memory of it happening; I can't relive it. I just remember it as a fact; it's something that I know happened.

I used to have a red-hot temper. My therapist even said I had plenty of good reasons for it. She pointed out that I've endured a lot of psychological abuse in my life, and what was actually a good sense of self-esteem had become overly sensitized. This has resulted in an extremely poor and dangerous response system. I wasn't a mean person; quite the contrary. Most people would describe me as a very nice man. And I think I really was a very nice young man. But when the wrong buttons were pushed, I could immediately switch into being a hot-tempered reactionary.

Through decades of emotional abuse about being homosexual, I had developed a red-hot core of rage that was covered over by a usually docile volcanic mountain of good-boy syndrome. My self-perceived faults, combined with my Southern heritage, were constantly demanding of me to not only be a good boy but, in fact, be good-er than most. I tried hard to fulfill my mother's dreams and "Be sweet." But as I aged, my triggers became more easily engaged, and these deep emotional habits of rage became more and more abrupt. To be healed of these outbursts, I had to break the habit of rage. I had to create in my brain new neural pathways for thinking, new actions, and new words. I had to learn to better define forgiveness and implement that new definition. I had to redesign the triggers of my rage and apply new actions when they were activated. I couldn't change the world; I had to change me.

Learning to pray naked is such a simple thing to do. I didn't say it's always easy. But it is always simple. It starts with observation. Eventually, it'll develop into a constant action of observation in your life instead of something that you continuously have to stop and purposefully do. Rediscovering the life force within you and deeply understanding it is the same life force that creates your world is a powerful, calming, and anxiety-reducing realization. You are not separate; you are connected. You're not a bubble of white-as-snow encapsulated spirit energy that's being forced to learn lessons by living in a materialistic, nonspiritual, evil world. Instead, this beautiful, expanding world that's all around you is actually all you. You are it; it is you. Even more profoundly, you can now realize you are It, and It is you. Please allow me a moment to quote John Lennon:

Imagine there's no heaven,
It's easy if you try.
No hell below us;
Above us only sky.
Imagine all the people
Living for today.
Ah

Imagine there's no countries,
It isn't hard to do.
Nothing to kill or die for
And no religion, too.

Imagine all the people
Living life in peace.

You may say I'm a dreamer,
But I'm not the only one.
I hope someday you'll join us
And the world will be as one.

In this book, I've given you an opportunity to see God in a different nonreligious light. Imagine if there were no religions and we simply sought the ever-apparent source of energy that surrounds us. This is what I've attempted to describe and how it expresses as us. I've introduced the idea of a Quantum Consciousness and how it expresses as you. I've also helped you understand the hypnotic nature of life itself and how religious fervor uses trance. I hope in Chapter 9 you started to really sense exactly how similar the concepts of self-hypnosis and prayer really are. At the end of Chapter 1, I wrote this:

"Who is the one person in the world you have the greatest power over?" The answer to that question has to be "You." You are the one and only person that you can truly control, modify, change, excite, calm, and transform." And then I asked you, "How?"

I feel silly even considering writing this down, but it's the truth, and it used to plague me every single morning. When I would pick up my hairdryer to tame the mane, I would go into this mindless, hair-drying trance and say in my mind the most horrible things about my father. It was like a tape recorder that would automatically begin. I'd cuss him and think about all the things I could have said to him. While I was welding that hairdryer, my round brush furiously straightening out all those curls that were just like his, in my mind, I'd be calling him horrible names. I know it sounds silly and looks even more silly in writing, but I did this without fail every single morning for decades, well into my adulthood. It wasn't a conscious decision; it was a trigger response from having a hairdryer in my hand. This emotional habit wasn't hurting my father in any way, but it was a self-inflicted paper cut to my psyche every single morning. I was doing it to myself. Why?

When I was growing up in the 1970s, feathered hair and the blow-dry look were what everyone did. My father insisted that blow-dryers were for girls, and I wasn't allowed to have one because, to him, only sissified boys would use one. So every day at 4 a.m., I'd wake up and take a shower, then would sneak into my mother's closet where there was an old-fashioned hairdryer. It was the kind that came in a plastic case that looked like a hatbox with a zipper around the top. It had an electric base with a fan and heater that attached to a flexible air hose, which delivered the hot air to a plastic bonnet at the end. Momma would use it to dry her hair when she put it up in rollers. I'd sneak that old hairdryer into my room, detach the bonnet and use the bare end of the flexible hose as a makeshift blow-dryer. Once my hair was blow-dried to high school perfection, I'd reattach the bonnet and put the dryer back in the case, then sneak it back into my mother's closet, placing it exactly as I'd found it. Then I'd go back to bed for a couple more hours of sleep before I got ready to get on the bus for school. I did this every morning throughout high school. You can imagine the things that were going through my head about my father as I did this daily ritual. It's a bit of an embarrassing story to tell, but I hope it helps you understand exactly how habitual emotions can become tied to a physical trigger.

Finally, in my forties, I was able to address this emotional habit and change the pattern. First, I had to acknowledge it and dig deep to remember where and when this pattern first began. Once I knew how far back it went, it was easy to see that it no longer was relevant to my morning ritual. But that didn't change the trigger.

I certainly wasn't emotionally ready to go in the opposite direction and say positive and loving things about my father during those three minutes of my day, but I did decide to start using those three minutes constructively. I wrote a simple affirmation of what I wanted my day to be like, taped it to my mirror, and every morning during that hair-drying trance, I'd quietly chant that positive affirmation into my stylish coiffure. It took decision, repeated choosing, failure, deciding again, starting again, and mindfulness to reach a successful place in life where now I just pick up a hairdryer only for one reason—to coif!

Brain science teaches us there are different sections of the brain that function separately but also together: reptile, mammal, and primate. The reptilian brain is focused on avoiding harm. It's commonly referred to as fight-or-flight. It avoids threats and approaches opportunities. The mammalian part of our brain focuses on rewards. It has an eye for things that maintain us, like food. The primate part of the brain gives us higher cerebral functions like problem-solving, tools, making mental maps of the world, connecting with others, time, and distance.

Published author and trusted psychologist, Dr. Rick Hanson, has provided a way to remember those three aspects of the brain. The reptilian brain is the lizard, the mammal brain is the mouse, and the primate brain is the monkey. Each brain has its moment when you have to either pet the lizard, feed the mouse, or hug the monkey.

When the lizard is overly excited, fear has us in its grips, and we want to fight or run. Deep breathing is a great way to pet the lizard. Decidedly engaging your parasympathetic nervous system to gain control over subconscious mind activity like heart rate and breathing rate will relax your lizard.

Becoming more mindful of your personal reward system is a great way to learn to properly feed the mouse. When I experience the great benefits of healthy food choices, I naturally want to consume better food. When I experience the benefits of clean air without smoke, I want to breathe more of it. The mouse responds quickly to the experience of benefits.

To hug the monkey, bring into your mind the feelings you have about a person that you know with absolute conviction loves you deeply. Someone that you know wants the best in life for you. At any time, in any situation, you can bring that person into mind and imagine them standing beside you. You can imagine the feeling of them putting their hand on your shoulder or allowing them to hug you. Your monkey mind will cuddle up to love when you let it.

All three of these actions—petting the lizard, feeding the mouse, and hugging the monkey—are forms of observation, and they are creative. As we now know, observation is the same thing as praying. We can use the act of observing to continue down a path we like, or we can use it to change directions and go down a different path.

I read a story about Jean Houston, one of the foremost voices in the human potential movement who has written and published a multitude of books. In the story, she talks about having a real phobia about writing a book. She also said that she had no doubt about her skills as a great cook. So she used her mental self-persona as a cook and would take all those skill sets and that level of self-confidence away from her stove and to her desk to do her writing. In doing so, she has managed to serve the entire world many wonderful "dishes" as books.

Her story made me think about my own career personas. I was an unabashedly confident singer and stage personality in my younger days. Sometimes I need to bring that persona into a situation and use the skills and perspective of that guy to solve a problem or accomplish a task. Because I felt so incredibly flawed for so many years, I also developed a very empathetic persona. Sometimes that empathy finds its way into the work I do now as a hypnotist. I have many other personas that I can employ, and each time I use them, it draws together new neural pathways in my own brain, allowing me new thoughts.

Remember, Donald Hebb from Chapter 8 taught us, "Neurons that fire together wire together." Taking one persona and superimposing its positive personality traits onto a different persona with a different set of skills is a powerful form of observation that's very creative. In this manner, you can continue to pray without ceasing.

Paul Levy, in his book *The Quantum Revelation*, describes this form of observation as a quantum blueprint. It's taking the things that you do naturally and with ease, the things you're good at, and giving credence to the self-identity that carries those qualities. Then you can superimpose that self-identity onto any other aspect of yourself that's facing a challenge. It's no secret that the feeling of being overwhelmed just creates more feelings of being overwhelmed. But confidence also creates more feelings of confidence, and the confidence you have in one activity can definitely be transferred to another activity in your life.

One of the great teachers of hypnosis, Jason Linett, uses this technique to create a state that he calls Peak Performance. It's a multiple-step technique that I teach in private sessions to create a sense of power in your life and tie that sense of power to a physical trigger. Using your imagination, you can practice that trigger release over and over until it becomes a natural response that is a powerful mental state creating good in your life. It'll function in the exact same way as a hairdryer did for me, but it'll create the opposite effect. Jason is famous for teaching his clients and students, "You're already using hypnosis; I'll just show you how to do it better."

Remember in Chapter 2 my encounter with Mrs. Brown on the church steps? After that story, I gave you a step-by-step description of praying naked and using quantum observation. Once she had made her remarks to me, I took the following steps:

1. I got to a safe place and started to breathe. You might say I was petting the lizard. I used my parasympathetic nervous system to my advantage instead of my disadvantage. Deep, slow breathing gave me control, and it will for you too. It creates a safe space in your body to recognize the truth of any perceived danger. Closing my eyes was not necessary, but since I was alone in my car, eye closure gave me the opportunity to shut down an unnecessary sensory perception and helped calm me even quicker.

From a hypnosis viewpoint, using these breathing techniques could be considered a form of induction. Specifically, this would be a progressive relaxation induction that took me into a light state of trance.

2. I started to smile. I took action to change the brain chemicals swirling in my head. I knew there were other chemicals—pleasure chemicals—at my disposal if I wanted them. I used a physical trigger built into my body by nature herself and flooded my brain. Yes, I was most definitely feeding the mouse. I was rewarding myself with personal control. Power is something we humans crave. Power is best used on yourself. When you know the power of your brain chemicals, you can use them.

A hypnotist might consider this a set of deepeners. Once in a light trance from the breathing exercises, I then used a physical trigger of smiling to utilize a more powerful state where I was pulling resources from stronger archetypes that already exist in me. This is what Jason Linett referred to as creating the peak performance state.

3. With my reason and logic now back intact, I made a decision. I knew I could feel shame if I wanted to, but I didn't want that. I knew I could feel hatred for her, but I also didn't want that. I wanted to feel something else. I decided pity was the best I could feel in that moment. I knew I could eventually move from pity to forgiveness with a little time and distance from the situation. So pity was where I chose to start. I felt pity for her ignorance. I felt pity for her to continue living in such a cage of systematic hate drawn from her church teaching and that she so eloquently maintained. And I chose to remember how kind she was to me as a young man. I chose to feel gratitude for her kindness in those days. You might interpret this as a version of the monkey hug. I allowed the kind and gentle version of Mrs. Brown that I knew from my high school years to just sit with me in silence. In hypnosis, I would call this the act of giving suggestions. I am in a self-induced trance state and actively breaking an emotional habit while also giving it a new set of neural pathways. When I was finished, I opened my eyes in an action of emerging.

This entire three step-action was a prayer. I never had to bow my head, call upon the name of the Lord, beg, or approach on bended knee; none of that. That religious clothing is unnecessary because I already know who I am. I am an individuated expression of Consciousness. Already know that I just decided to observe something new. It would be illogical of me to call out to God as if It were in some distant place watching. Illogical because God is All. God, Quantum Consciousness, the infinitely intelligent and energized molecular space surrounding me and composing me is also the very composition of the car I was sitting in and the air surrounding me. It is all me, and It is also Mrs. Brown. I am God. She is God. We are God. We are all expressions of a singular Quantum Consciousness that has individuated into our personal expressions of It. And we get to choose how It responds and acts on an individuated level. Mrs. Brown and I chose differently.

Here is a clear starting point for praying naked. Define and then believe in what you are. I'm not talking about your personality traits or habits, your value systems, your star sign, your DNA, or anything physical. Understand what you are—a creation of individuated infinity—to such a degree that you rarely ever have to stop again and declare it. Just know it and believe it to your core. The name you choose doesn't matter. You can call yourself a "child of God," "individuated Consciousness," "the Universe personified,"or a "child of Christ" whatever is comfortable to you. Just own it to such a degree that you never have to rethink it; you simply live it. Own your power as that creation.

Your every thought is already a prayer. Some of your thoughts are more focused and powerful than others, but they're all creative to some degree because that is your nature and you are that powerful. Own it. Take responsibility for your life, what you say, and what you continuously think about. All these are forms of observation that are creating your world. Don't be afraid that you caught yourself thinking poorly about someone or something; simply own it. Then switch directions and think good. Consciously decide to think more good thoughts than bad. Catch yourself judging others, and then instead of scolding yourself, laugh at your own hypocrisy! Be your friend and pet your lizard when he needs it. Feed your mouse. Hug your monkey. Doing that alone is life-changing. Learning to consciously exercise your own power in your everyday experiences provides you with the ability to beautifully paint your world with meaning and excitement.

Gain more and more control over your body. Your body has systems that function in specific ways, and it should be no mystery to you as to how they work. Be curious! There is an entire internet, and there are books upon books in libraries that are at your very fingertips. All of them explain your breathing and heart rate, the power of stretching your muscles, and the benefits of eating healthy and exercising. When you do this, you are observing your body. You are creating and recreating. All these things are forms of prayer—prayer that is naked. This is how you can begin today praying naked. These prayers have no religious cloth whatsoever. Knowing your body and how it works becomes a function of observation for you to observe the good in your body instead of being singularly focused on the problems associated with aging. How much of your body is still functioning properly? Focus on that! It's time we stop begging God for health while also refusing to stop eating the things causing us poor health. Observe.

Learn to breathe. The conscious act of breathing is so much more than the level of breathing done by the subconscious mind, which merely keeps us alive. Breathing is an expression and a decision. Breathing is joy. Breathing is both calm and elation. It can be euphoria and bliss. Breathing is life. Learn the difference between breathing for energy and for emergency. In just the simple act of breathing differently, you'll feel different because you're behaving differently.

It takes effort to clear out old neural pathways that have become habitual in nature and build new ones. But the good news is that the new ones are built the same way the old ones were. Old neural pathway habits were built by little singular moments, and so are new ones. You can tear down old bitter habits by responding in a singular chosen moment of happiness, choosing love more and more repeatedly, and utilizing the wisdom you already possess.

Here's one last very simple observation that's equally as powerful as it is simple. You can take a straightforward and positive fact and turn it into a deliciously positive experience. Look for positive facts that surround you—a really cute child with a sweet face. Turn that fact about a face into a sweet and wonderful experience. Savor that child's face and presence. When you smell a bakery, turn that moment into something decadently delicious, even if you are on a calorie-restricted diet. Enjoy the smell of the bakery instead of cursing it because smelling those calories won't put an ounce of weight on you. Someone held the door open for you at the supermarket. For just a second, relish in that person's kindness. Be grateful for it and look for an opportunity to pass it on. This is observation, and it is powerful. Looking for and recognizing the good around you is praying naked.

Émile Coué was a French pharmacist born in the mid-1800s. He noticed that when he gave medications to his patients and also pointed out all the benefits of taking the drugs, his patients got better quicker than if he just handed them the medication with no praise. He believed that somehow his positive suggestions about the medications allowed his patients to have a better experience taking them. He would give his patients a very simple mantra to say while taking their medication, "Every day, in every way, I'm getting better and better." This is praying naked.

Chapter 12

In Conclusion

Finding a meaningful and satisfying way to feel connected to this amazing ball of blue floating in space and living a life of significance from a perspective of higher function and value can be difficult in today's world. If you were born and educated in a traditional religious background like I was, what I have presented in this book may be a little bit different in terms of your approach to God. This approach is spiritual in nature, yet at the same time, it leans heavily into science and draws meaning from the material world around us.

In the first chapter of this book, I asked you a question: "Who is the one person in the world you have the greatest power over?" I've done my best to illustrate that the answer really is you. My aim was to demonstrate that you have built inside you the tools to change your life into an experience filled with meaning and awe. I set out to explain in simple terms that your brain is a wonderful tool always at your disposal to create. It's malleable and gives you tremendous control over nearly every aspect of you. You are the one and only person that can truly control, modify, change, excite, calm, and transform you. You are the one who chooses words, and you can choose new words that will develop into your reality. It is you who forms physical and emotional habits that become unconscious in nature and automatically express themselves without your conscious decision or permission. You have so much more control than you ever dreamed possible. Now you know... so what will you do now?

I was born into a farming family in the buckle most section of the Bible belt. I was told I needed to be healed, and I could be healed of a birth affliction—homosexuality. In quiet life-threatening desperation, I did everything I possibly knew to do in order to change who I was. I sought healing through an infinite number of bible studies, church groups, and a religious education which eventually led to a career as a Southern Baptist minister. When my "sexual defect" was finally discovered, I was thrown away, disowned by many of my family and friends, and kicked out of my religion. For that last part—being kicked out of my religion—I eventually became very grateful because it freed me and released me into a greater expression of life.

I was left with nothing to my name except an exceptional musical talent. My ability to sing got me through life and opened doors for me to financially take care of myself, but it never filled the void that had been left by the spiritual quest nurtured in me by a perceived defect. The adversity of being a homosexual had given rise in me a need to seek a theological system in which I could feel loved. When the time was right, and my heart was open, my teachers were standing right in front of me.

Step-by-step, teacher by teacher, philosophy by philosophy, book by book, I transformed. I found healing in study, devotion, meditation, prayer-treatment, hypnosis, and quantum observation. Today I feel fulfilled and happy about my life. I'm still changing, always growing, and learning to love in deeper and more fulfilling ways. I am always observing. And I have great conviction and awe-filled expectation that I will continue to grow in love until I drop dead in my tracks—hopefully quickly and without notice on a beautiful mountain trail or water-skiing at the age of one hundred and three. If I could put a laughing emoji in a book, I would place it here.

I grew up feeling very alone and singled out. I now know I am not alone in this great and wonderful world of change. I've seen people with crippling anxiety grow into lives of calm and peace. I've watched people with phobias and fears so strong they were disabled in majorly important areas of life: modes of transportation, weight, health, speaking publicly, smoking, and just being able to go to the dentist. I've seen gay people find peace in their lives and health in their partner choices. I've seen people from all walks of life give up emotional habits that were destroying their lives through unconscious and automatic behaviors. I've seen such a reversal of life's dilemmas that, in religious circles, they would have been called miracles.

For many of you, this is a first look into a new kind of theology that utilizes all the wisdom of the ancient teachings, keeps the mysticism and mystery, and gives space for magical moments in life that are seemingly miraculous while also moving away from the dogma of fear, superstition, and incantations so wordy and meaningless they've been relegated to "thoughts and prayers." This kind of theology that I present here is inclusive for all people and is based on the energy of love and only love. It's not a doctrine of a God who is jealous, angry, sometimes good, and partially evil.

My theological view of Quantum Consciousness gives all God-seekers of every expression a strong cornerstone to build their lives upon, and even those who have called themselves atheists have a scientific approach that connects them to their world and other life forms. Quantum Mind explains the oneness of all our thinking, dreaming, intuition, and profound connection. This is a theology lacking condemnation and giving you all the room you need to consider life after death and decide for yourself if there is a hereafter. No one has a definitive answer that comes from science or experience as to a heaven, hell, or empty nothingness. You get to decide what you believe and how it motivates you to live your best life. Morality comes very simply. "Love your neighbor as yourself" is present in every theological system. It must be the truth of being.

I have given you a grand reason to cherish your body and especially your brain. It's a powerful tool that's malleable to your experience and provides you with the opportunity to create an incredible life through observation. You do not need permission to create a more meaningful life by seeing, feeling, intuiting, believing, imagining, and expecting as much as you want. This is basic to your very nature.

If I could tell you to do one thing right this second, it would be to start observing. Your eyes are already open, so use them. Your ears are already listening; use them. You have personalities and personas that carry your best skills. Your emotions are fully functioning, ready, and engaged. They have a direct connection to your imagination, and together, all these things make a team of powerful creators. Start using your team for what you want.

Life is hypnotic in nature. Harnessing that hypnotic power and natural state of trance and using it as a form of prayer that continues without ceasing is yours for the taking if you simply realize it and put it to your good use instead of your detriment.

Our every thought is energy that's used as a creative force toward a general outcome. Because of the depth of emotion that's attached to thought, some are more powerful than others. Prayer is also thought. But prayerful thought is powerfully energized toward the movement of energy for a specific outcome. Observation can also be powerfully energized toward a specific outcome, and so is hypnosis.

Your every thought is naked. It's not dressed in religious clothing. You can pray naked, and it's powerful.

Pray naked.